CONTENTS

KU-116-015

DEDICATION

This book is dedicated to my wife, Margaret, and sons, Steven and Mark, who heard nothing but marketing and sales talk for over a year and still provided support and encouragement.

ACKNOWLEDGEMENTS

The research for this book was conducted over a number of years – I visited many hospitality units, and only once was I refused assistance, and that was from someone not directly employed in the industry.

Marketing and sales personnel took time out from their busy schedules to provide information, while many owner operators and managers provided interviews and data (not all of which I have been able to include directly within the text). I should like to acknowledge all those who assisted, in particular, the following (not listed in any order):

I Anderson, Solihull Swallow Hotel; I Lamaison, Granada Studio Tours Ltd; P Leith, Leith's Good Food; H Taylor, Edwardian Hotels; S Elsdon, Banqueting & Conference Sales Executive; J Maltby, Toby Restaurants; R Ward, Wards Breweries; C Thomas, Telephone Sales Trainer; A Coby, Computer Systems Consultant; S Tweed, Consort Hotels; P Roberts, Distinctly Different; R Harwood, Rutland Hotel, South Yorkshire; P Keary, Elton Hotel; S Dorman, American Express; J Jenkinson, Evesham Hotel; Don and Samantha Horton, Ebford House Hotel; Z Chaudhry, Bella Pasta Restaurant, Nottingham; D Bowie, Belmont Marketing; E Holden; E Marsh, Cavendish Hotel, Derbyshire; I Holdsworth, Swallow Regional Sales Executive; Hotel & Restaurant Magazine; P Baker, Stoke-on-Trent Moat House; P Ord, Corporate Sales Manager, Cumberland Hotel; E Roberts, North Wales Tourist Board; R Collings, Green Lawns Hotel, Falmouth; B Shaw, Bradby Club, Chesterfield; Fortes Hotels; C Mayes, Cumberland Hotel, London; Skills & Enterprise Unit, Department of Employment; J Duffield, ABM Catering Ltd; L Dicken, Broadgate Club, London; N Bellone, Sedgebrook Hall; Department of Trade & Industry; Campanile Hotels (UK) Ltd; M Ford Photography, South Yorkshire; Hilton National Hotels; Swallow Hotels Ltd.

Sincere thanks and gratitude additionally to Liz Woffenden who painstakingly corrected drafts and typed the script.

INTRODUCTION

This book is designed to introduce readers to the fascinating and challenging area of hospitality marketing and sales. It opens with an outline of the industry and sections on general marketing and sales, and continues by describing the importance of effective planning before dealing in more depth with specific marketing and sales methods.

Within such an introductory text it is not possible to cover all the aspects of hospitality marketing to the depth certain readers may require. However, by utilising the key points listed at the end of each chapter and the assignments and exercises provided in Appendix A, readers will be able to extend their knowledge and skills considerably.

The research for this text was carried out over several years, with a concentration of investigation in the months prior to its completion. The aim was to provide practical insight into current marketing and sales practice rather than detailed explanations of more theoretical approaches.

The hospitality industry has had some notable marketing and sales successes, yet it remains criticised by some for a lack of sustained effort in some areas. Whatever the real situation, a study of marketing and sales activity is a challenging one as, while there exists certain commonality in respect to approach, there also exists an increasing divergence.

The industry currently suffers (like many other industries) from a general reduction in demand, an increase in competition and alterations to the nature of demand from an increasingly sophisticated market.

In periods of decline and expansion, positive marketing and sales will assist operators in maintaining and developing profitable business. However, such activities do not solve all the problems and are only one part – albeit an increasingly important part – of the exciting business of hospitality provision.

If by providing this text I assist both the reader and the industry, then I will have achieved one of the main aims in compiling it.

I hope you enjoy reading it, obtain both new knowledge and skills and, when the opportunity arises, give back some of these benefits to the customer without whom there would be no industry.

HOW TO USE THIS TEXT

This text is designed to take readers through some of the more theoretical concepts of marketing and sales, and then move through more practical, action-related practices.

Each chapter is provided with:

- an introduction;
- a summary or review;
- key points;
- related questions.

By reading this section first, elements of each chapter should become clearer. Additionally, in Appendix A, there are a number of assignments and exercises that relate specifically to each chapter. Upon completion of a chapter, you may wish to attempt either the assignment or one of the exercises, which are designed to provide you with additional learning and, I hope, satisfaction. However, as with all such disciplines, there exists a high degree of interrelation and wherever appropriate I have included references to related factors appearing elsewhere within the text.

Readers with some degree of understanding of this subject may wish to undertake all the assignments and exercises outlined in Appendix A. If they possess part responsibility for the function of marketing and sales within their workplace, they may find that the completion of the assignments brings with it not only increased understanding of the subject but also increased business!

Excluding the references to individuals within the industry, I have included no reference within chapters to other reading material. This is in no way a slight to the authors of other texts on marketing and sales, rather it is my attempt to identify activities the hospitality industry utilises.

Throughout the book, certain marketing and sales terminology is used; while I have attempted to keep jargon phrases to a minimum, there is a definite need for their inclusion. Readers coming across an unfamiliar phrase are directed to Appendix B.

CHAPTER ONE

INTRODUCTION TO HOSPITALITY MARKETING

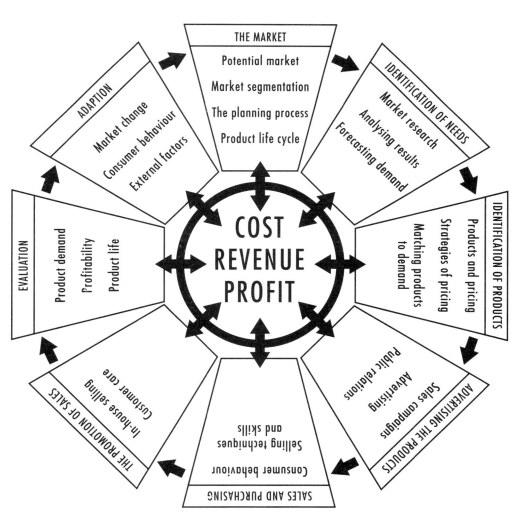

THE MARKET
- Potential market
- Market segmentation
- The planning process
- Product life cycle

IDENTIFICATION OF NEEDS
- Market research
- Analysing results
- Forecasting demand

IDENTIFICATION OF PRODUCTS
- Products and pricing
- Strategies of pricing
- Matching products to demand

ADVERTISING THE PRODUCTS
- Sales campaigns
- Advertising
- Public relations

SALES AND PURCHASING
- Consumer behaviour
- Selling techniques and skills

THE PROMOTION OF SALES
- In-house selling
- Customer care

EVALUATION
- Product demand
- Profitability
- Product life

ADAPTION
- Market change
- Consumer behaviour
- External factors

COST REVENUE PROFIT

Fig. 1.1   THIS DIAGRAM ILLUSTRATES THE SALES AND MARKETING ACTIVITY CYCLE

INTRODUCTION

This chapter concerns itself with the role and importance of marketing and sales to the hospitality industry. It includes sections on the background to marketing and sales, definitions of the hospitality industry and will identify in general terms the types of markets the industry is involved with.

> Pru Leith, owner of a large and highly successful catering business: 'Positive sales and marketing activity is something all operators should be involved in. It is an aspect the industry does not do enough of and it is often the area many companies reduce in times of recession. It is when business is difficult that sales and marketing activities should increase.'

The section on products will look at the tangible products and services the industry offers and the less tangible including relaxation and comfort.

The section on marketing relevance will identify how particular sectors, that is, hotels, restaurants, motorway services and fast-food operators, make use of marketing and sales activities to assist customer satisfaction and business growth.

The section on the marketing and sales function provides an overview of how companies organise such activities. It describes the roles and responsibilities of marketing and sales personnel and explains the use of other agencies.

The points raised in this chapter are in many cases not specific to the hospitality industry. There is relevance to many other industries. It is the hospitality industry's speciality of providing service, not 'products', that marks it out for special attention.

LEARNING OBJECTIVES

By working through this chapter, completing questions and reviewing the key points, readers will be able to:

- Provide a definition of the term 'hospitality industry'.
- Have an appreciation of the industry's contribution to the economy.
- Understand the basic role of marketing and sales in identifying and satisfying customer needs, and maintaining and improving business.
- Identify and classify the various sectors of the industry.
- Identify in general terms the markets the industry seeks to serve.
- Identify the range and style of products the industry provides.
- Explain the general differences in approach to marketing and sales by the various sectors of the industry.
- Have an understanding of how marketing and sales activity is operated.

THE HOSPITALITY INDUSTRY

The description and definition of the industry sector which provides food, drink, accommodation and leisure facilities has altered throughout its long history. The most widely accepted description up until a few years ago was the hotel and catering industry, which for many omitted the many operators who were involved in tourist, leisure and recreation provision.

A DEFINITION OF HOSPITALITY INDUSTRY
Hospitality: 'Friendly and generous reception and service of guests'.
Industry: 'Diligence'.
Source: *Oxford Current English Dictionary.*

For operators in the 1990s, the term 'hospitality' creates a more positive and customer-friendly image; the sector is concerned not only with providing food, drink and accommodation, but also with service and opportunities for leisure and relaxation. The industry does not deal with products such as soap powder, lawn mowers or drills. The emphasis is on the total package, the product plus the benefits to the customer. This is covered in more detail in the following sections.

THE INDUSTRY AND ITS EFFECT ON THE ECONOMY

A considerable amount of material has been written about the industry, its size, economic contribution and make up. The move in the UK away from a manufacturing-based economy to a more service-based economy has been a recognisable trend for a number of decades. Disregarding the fluctuations of the UK and world economy and their effect on the industry, hospitality operators provide an important contribution to the country's economic performance (see Figure 1.2 on page 12).

It is important to appreciate that the figure of £25.2 billion spent on tourism in the UK in 1990 represents direct spending, and does not take into account the individuals and companies indirectly supported by this spend.

'The hospitality industry has been one of the fastest growing areas of employment throughout the last ten years. [See Figure 1.3 on page 12.] Between June 1980 and June 1990 the number of jobs in the industry increased by 309,000. The number of employees in sectors related to the industry grew by 25 per cent between June 1981 and June 1991 compared to an increase of just over 1 per cent for all employees in all industries. In June 1990 the industry employed directly over 1.5 million people. With some job losses over the last year (1991), the industry is forecasted to continue expanding, with skills shortages being the biggest constraint on its development.'

Source: Skills and Enterprise Briefing, November 1991.

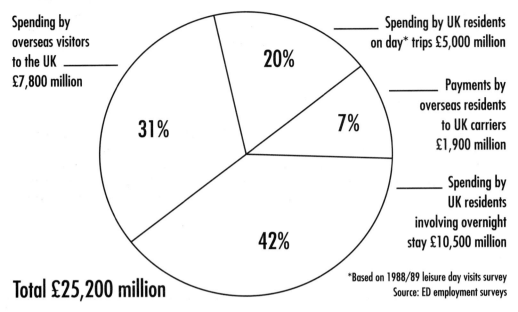

Spending by overseas visitors to the UK £7,800 million

Spending by UK residents on day* trips £5,000 million

Payments by overseas residents to UK carriers £1,900 million

Spending by UK residents involving overnight stay £10,500 million

20%

7%

31%

42%

Total £25,200 million

*Based on 1988/89 leisure day visits survey
Source: ED employment surveys

Fig. 1.2
TOURISM SPENDING IN THE UK IN 1990, PER CENT

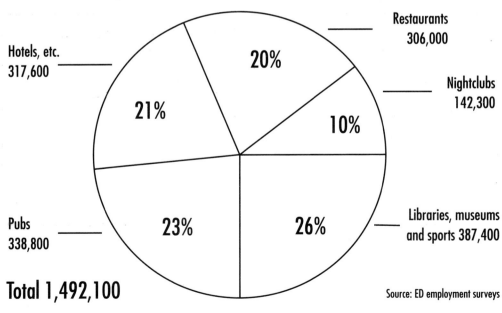

Hotels, etc.
317,600

Restaurants
306,000

Nightclubs
142,300

Libraries, museums and sports 387,400

Pubs
338,800

20%

21%

10%

23%

26%

Total 1,492,100

Source: ED employment surveys

Fig. 1.3
EMPLOYEES EMPLOYED IN TOURISM-RELATED INDUSTRIES IN GREAT BRITAIN IN JUNE 1990

Compared with tourism, the breakdown of hospitality operators and units is difficult to establish, due in part to changes in the industrial classification published by HMSO and the structural diversity of the industry. It is sufficient for this text to identify the various sectors within the hospitality industry and their relative size.

THE STRUCTURE OF THE INDUSTRY

As already identified it is difficult to outline distinct sectors due to the diversity of hospitality provision. The grouping or placing of units into sectors will obviously depend on the factors taken into consideration. The relationship of the various sectors to their particular markets and the subsequent range and style of marketing and sales activity is the basis on which I have structured the sectors (see Figure 1.4 below).

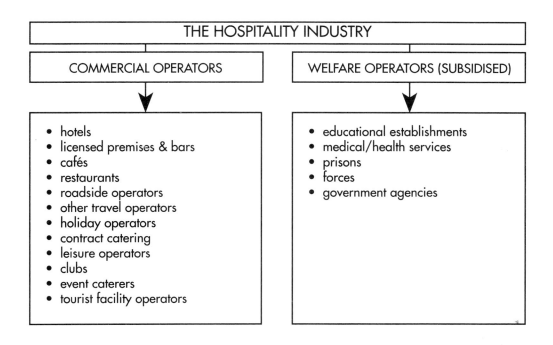

Fig. 1.4
THE STRUCTURE OF THE HOSPITALITY INDUSTRY

COMMERCIAL AND WELFARE

The separation identified in Figure 1.4 would possibly indicate that marketing and sales activity would in the main occur within the commercial sector. On the face of it, welfare operations, by the very nature of their provision, would neither be concerned with identifying market need, nor be involved in serious promotional activity. This, however, is not the case. For example, the decline in school meal provision and take up has been well documented, so has the marketing and sales initiatives that the school meals service and other contractors have undertaken, including themed meals, promotional comparison and alteration to facilities. The 1980 Education Act (which removed the right of all but the neediest of children to have a school meal) and the Local Government Act 1986 (putting all school catering contracts out for tender) proved an incentive for progressive operators to make use of marketing and sales activities. This perhaps is a classical example of how the change in the market encouraged a positive and effective marketing response. This is a trend that can be identified throughout the welfare sector.

It is also apparent upon investigation that it is too simplistic to group all hotels or all licensed premises within the same sector. All the sectors within both main groups will have varying approaches to marketing and sales activity.

Therefore, taken from the viewpoint of marketing and sales, we need to differentiate between the type of operations to identify the relation of marketing activity. The hospitality industry is an extremely diverse one, and this diversity of structure leads to a diversity of approaches to marketing and sales concepts, strategy, planning and practice.

The main difference between the two main sectors is the type of relationship each has with the customer. Within the welfare sector the client is often captive, that is, there exists only one provision and it is an inherent part of other services, for example, education or health care. Marketing and sales activities would then be generally aimed at monitoring or increasing take up. Advertising, costly promotional activity and the use of professional marketing agencies are not common.

Within the commercial sector, the client is generally not 'captive', that is, there is a major element of choice through competition. Therefore, marketing and sales activity has to be more aggressive.

PRODUCT MARKETING VERSUS BENEFIT MARKETING

While I have indicated that the marketing emphasis within the welfare sector is changing, the main approach may be characterised as product orientated, that is, marketing and selling the product, the food, drink or service. The commercial sector has changed drastically to a benefit marketing approach – moving marketing and sales activity away from the product and towards the customer.

CONCLUSION

The structure of today's hospitality industry is in part an outcome of the relation between the operators and their markets. Marketing and sales activities reflect the structure of the market and the structure of the market affects the manner in which such activities take place. The industry offers a diverse range of products, services and facilities, reflecting the potential demand for such provision.

The following sections will look in more depth at the arguments for effective marketing, the make up of the hospitality market and how the industry puts together its packages of products.

THE RELEVANCE OF MARKETING AND SALES

Preceding sections have identified the importance of the hospitality industry to the economy and how the structure of the industry is affected by potential market demand.

This section is concerned within identifying the factors behind the increasing use and sophistication of marketing and sales activity within the industry. Although some would argue that the average 5–6 per cent on turnover spent by the industry is insufficient in today's business climate.

'Scepticism remains rampant in the industry on the benefits of marketing our product. How else can you explain the low advertising spend in the industry? Miniscule by comparison with the manufacturers and retailers of this world, there's the almost non-existent expenditure on research. Ironic really, considering our entire business is based upon the satisfaction of our guests. How can we satisfy them if we don't know what they want?'
Source: Hugh Taylor, Sales and Marketing Director, Edwardian Hotels.

WHAT IS MARKETING?

As you work through this text you will see that marketing and sales is not a complete function, rather a variety of related activities. While there exist many definitions, I prefer the following:

'Marketing is the management process for identifying and satisfying customer needs profitably.'
Source: Chartered Institute of Marketing.

You will find aspects of this definition repeated throughout this text: I have always considered that it is with the practical utilisation of effective methods to increase business where the emphasis should lie, not with theoretical concepts.

> 'Marketing is not an elusive art, it is more a science of identifying customer needs and wants and presenting a package that answers these needs.'
> Source: Hugh Taylor, Edwardian Hotels.

Marketing then should not be a reactive activity, but a pro-active activity designed to assist the industry and its customers. Let us look at this reactive approach in more detail.

REACTIVE MARKETING

In the main, hospitality operators are concerned with profit. While some may state publicly, 'we are here to provide a service', or 'our aim is to satisfy our customers', without profit they could not continue to function. Reactive marketing is characterised by a response to reducing a fall in profits. This was clearly evident in the early part of the 1990s when reduction in demand, due to such international factors as economic recession, saw many operators go out of business. Marketing and sales activities centred on a response to a rapidly changing market. Hospitality operators utilised sales activities in an attempt to maintain business. Marketing and sales activity was (and still is in some cases) characterised by 'blitz' campaigns, price reductions and operational cost-cutting.

In extreme cases, this short-term strategy may appear attractive or, at least, the best option. This was the case in the late 1980s following the American air raid on Libya, and in 1991 preceding and following the Gulf War. The huge reduction in demand from the USA, especially for hotel accommodation in London, saw hotels drastically reducing prices, laying off staff and cutting costs. Aggressive marketing and sales activity was utilised then in an attempt to maintain demand.

In times of recession, many hospitality operators find themselves re-embracing marketing and sales in the short term, having neglected such activity when business was booming.

> RELEVANCE FACTOR 1
> Hospitality operators utilise marketing and sales activities in a reaction to reductions in demand.

The reduction of prices to attract customers in periods of recession is a risk strategy and one that many operators will resist.

'Despite reduced demand for our à la carte menu, we decided that to reduce prices would result in a reduction in quality for the customer. The restaurant has become well known for the quality of its food and beverage provision establishing a lead position within the area. To have reduced standards would have been an unacceptable strategy.'
Source: Robert Collings, Director, Greens Lawns Hotel and Restaurant.

However, hospitality operators who utilise only this reactive strategy may find business recovery is only short term.

RELEVANCE FACTOR 2
Positive and effective marketing is a long-term activity – designed to assist operators identify potential markets and sales opportunities.

IDENTIFYING MARKETS

In looking at the structure of the industry I identified that, while we may group types of operations together, that is, hotels or restaurants, there exist many differences. A restaurant offering up-market food and beverages at high prices will obviously differ to a fast-food style high street unit offering a standard food range. Both may offer quality food and service, but by the nature of the unit be targeted at different types of customer.

Hospitality operators seek to identify potential markets, that is, groups of potential customers. These may be tourists, families, conference facility users, the business trade, the young, the old and the Japanese. Once identified, these markets or groups will express particular buying potential and characteristics. When such groups are identified, the operator will seek further information about their particular needs.

RELEVANCE FACTOR 3
Effective marketing assists existing and potential operators to identify market groups who may have particular needs.

Note: this aspect is dealt with in more detail in Chapter 2 and in 'The industry and its products' (below).

IDENTIFYING CUSTOMER NEEDS

Once market groups have been identified, the operator will want to identify the particular needs, requirements and preferences of the potential customers. What type of product or service do they require or are willing to purchase? What is the best price structure that will attract them? Are their needs short or long term? Without identifying market potential and needs, operators may find themselves with empty restaurants, unfilled beds and under-utilised facilities.

RELEVANCE FACTOR **4**
Effective marketing assists the operator in identifying the particular needs, potential and purchasing preferences of targeted customers.

This aspect is dealt with in more detail in Chapter 3, 'Methods of identifying demand', and in Chapter 4, 'Telephone selling'.

FORECASTING DEMAND AND PLANNING FACILITIES

The operator will seek to identify and forecast demand for products, services or facilities. Identified low demand may cause the operator to alter the range of 'products' to better unit potential demand. Additionally, the operator may utilise marketing techniques and processes to analyse existing 'products' in an attempt to forecast alteration in demand. Wider factors are also taken into consideration, analysing not only the product, but also its style, location and access. A much quoted adage concerning success in planning was by an American hotelier who stated: 'There's only four things to consider when opening an hotel: location, location, location and location.'

RELEVANCE FACTOR **5**
By analysing competitors, by identifying potential demand and by seeking out the type of demand, operators can more effectively change "product ranges" or create new ones.

RAISING AWARENESS – SELLING AND PROMOTION

As identified in 'The structure of the industry' (above) there is a decrease in marketing and sales activity when the customer has little or no choice. For the majority of operators this is not the case, and they will need to create awareness of their 'products' within targeted markets. Operators will need to ensure that not only are potential customers aware of particular products, but also be aware of the benefits of their products against those of their competitors. The need is for fairly aggressive selling, reaching out to markets and customers, promoting their particular units, products, services and facilities.

RELEVANCE FACTOR **6**
Marketing and sales activities, such as advertising, telephone sales, promotional events and product packages, assist in both raising awareness in potential customers and encouraging change in purchasing behaviour.

This is dealt with in more detail in Chapter 4.

SATISFYING CUSTOMER NEEDS PROFITABLY

A busy unit or facility is not necessarily a profitable one. The product itself may be wrong, or the costs in providing the product, packaging it and promoting it may be too high. By conducting analysis on the type of business, its origin, costs and forecasted duration, the operator can identify the real nature of his or her business and its profitability.

> RELEVANCE FACTOR 7
> Marketing and sales activity can exercise control over business, identifying actual costs against revenue and indicate the level of customer satisfaction or dissatisfaction.

ADAPTING TO MARKET CHANGE

While the hospitality industry does not suffer the rapid demand change so characteristic of the toy or record industries, operators are affected by alterations in consumer demand.

Markets will decline rapidly or slowly, and consumers may demand increased sophistication or become price sensitive. New markets may emerge, for instance, the building of a new housing estate may bring increased business to a local public house with an associated demand for bar snacks. Or, on a larger scale, the growth in a particular market may force operators to adopt new marketing and selling activities. The increase in the number of individuals of pensionable age with increased disposable income has seen many operators target this particular growth market.

> RELEVANCE FACTOR 8
> Analysis of market change will assist the operator in identifying and satisfying emerging markets, thereby maintaining or improving business.

CONCLUSION

Hospitality operators in the main do not offer 'products', but rather a range of goods, services, facilities and benefits. For the operator to maintain and increase profitable business, there needs to be an awareness of what demand exists and what the demand is for.

The operator needs to be constantly reviewing the business, analysing sales and costs, identifying possible threats and opportunities.

The utilisation of the variety of effective marketing and sales activities assists this process and contributes in an increasingly positive way to the success of the business.

> 'The key factors that will affect the relevance of marketing and sales in the next decade are:
>
> - The hospitality industry is in the middle of a fundamental structural change, the outcome of which no one can predict with any certainty.
> - The over supply of bedrooms and hotels which were developed in the boom years of the mid- and late 1980s will continue to depress occupancies and achieved room rates for several years.
> - The changing trends in consumer taste, which continue to drive the market.
> - The challenge from external market forces, for example, firms cutting back on overnight accommodation to save on travel expenses or new technologies, such as satellite conferencing, changing the way how companies communicate.
> - More sophisticated use of technology in marketing and sales.
>
> These factors suggest that the current fierce competitive environment will continue. Although some companies have cut back on sales teams, the better groups and independents will need to make the best possible use of their marketing and sales resources to remain competitive in a volatile market place. Indeed, some experts suggest that without an effective marketing strategy, a company will not survive into the next decade.'
> Source: David Bowie, Belmont Marketing.

Readers may wish to refer to the sections given above before moving on to the next section, which concentrates in more detail on the make up and characteristics of the hospitality market.

MARKETS AND CUSTOMERS

In the preceding sections within this chapter, I have identified the structure of the industry and how it utilises marketing and sales activities to identify and satisfy customer needs profitably. Reference was made to the various groups and types of operators and how they attempt to provide products, services and facilities that will attract customers. This section will look in more detail at the market for the hospitality industry and the range of customer or client groups or segments. Such analysis is important as particular markets will exhibit certain buying characteristics which will affect the overall level of potential business. Additionally, customers are individuals and the hospitality operator needs to understand what motivates individuals to purchase.

All hospitality operators need to identify:

- the type of market(s) they are seeking to serve;
- the potential needs of the particular market (or markets);
- the factors that will encourage customers to utilise their premises, that is, location, quality and need;
- the factors that will prevent customers from utilising their premises, that is, lack of facilities, cost and awareness.

Therefore, detailed knowledge of the potential markets and the factors that will attract and maintain profitable business is of vital importance.

HOSPITALITY MARKETS

The market for the hospitality industry is vast and, despite fluctuations in the economy, has been increasing rapidly over the past few decades.

THE IDENTIFICATION AND SEPARATION OF MARKETS

Hospitality operators attempt to identify and separate particular markets, that is, groups of potential customers who possess recognisable common buying behaviour. This separation or, as it is often referred to, segmentation allows the planners to look more closely at any recognisable trend. The separation and classification of market groups has been actively pursued by various agencies over the years.

Market groups can be classified simply as:

COMMERCIAL OR BUSINESS

This comprises groups or individuals from companies and organisations seeking accommodation, conference, meeting, exhibition facilities and food and beverages.

For many operators, this market has been their prime target with an expansion of units in, or close to, city and commercial centres. Facilities, products and services have been extended in an attempt to satisfy what many operators have identified as an extremely profitable market group. Hotels in the boom period of the mid- to late 1980s were satisfied with a Monday to Thursday business, and many saw no reason to identify and satisfy the needs of other groups. The situation in the early 1990s has seen many of these operators recognise the problem of over dependence on one particular market group. While considerable marketing activity is still targeted at the business market, the general trend is of an overall reduction in demand, which may continue for some time to come.

TOURIST TRADE

The growth in tourism over the past two decades has seen many operators increase their marketing and sales activities related to attracting both UK and foreign tourists. Characteristics of this market are its diversity in type of customers and the trend towards 'packages'. UK tourists are increasing on average their number of stays in hotels and inns, but the stays are now of a shorter duration.

The UK has always attracted a considerable number of foreign tourists for a variety of reasons. The demands that certain national groups can make are considerable, due in part to the differing levels of expectation in respect of facilities and service. In general terms, tourist numbers from the USA are declining, while tourists from other countries are increasing the number of visits. Over the past few years, some hotels have undertaken considerable activity in an attempt to attract and satisfy the Japanese visitor.

Whether the opening of the Channel tunnel in 1993 will radically alter the foreign tourist market remains to be seen.

These two market groups have long been seen as the major ones for the majority of operators, and while each expresses certain common characteristics, they remain in reality increasingly diverse.

OTHER TYPES OF MARKET GROUPINGS

Additionally, operators will need to identify the needs of a variety of other groups, and the classification of these and the identification of their buying characteristics is problematic.

Consider the following possible groups – they are not meant in any way to be discriminating:

- pensioners;
- business women;
- travel groups, for example, coach tours;
- young adults;
- couples;
- local families;
- business men;
- exhibition organisers;
- the disabled;
- local associations;
- special-interest groups.

The list is endless and the variety of specialised needs and related demand difficult to ascertain.

Operators may have representatives of all the above groups using their premises within a given period, which, while in some respects encouraging, does bring with it its own problems. Careful handling is required by the operator in order to ensure an appropriate business mix. For example, at a Midlands hotel recently there were:

- A considerable number of families on a weekend break package.
- A large group of severely disabled people with friends and helpers.
- A group of businessmen at the end of a three-day company conference (all determined to enjoy the annual get together).

The hotel's staff dealt extremely well with the varying demands and needs of the three distinctly different groups. Excitable children from the 'weekenders' took over the leisure facility, while the businessmen took over the bar. The disabled group required assistance with access, while the older weekenders wanted to relax and enjoy quiet meals. A challenging weekend for the hotel and one they handled with quality customer care.

This identifies another method of grouping market groups, and that is by their buying behaviour or utilisation of products and facilities. A hotel could have the following groups on its premises:

- locals making use of the public bar;
- Saturday night dinner/dance groups;
- conference and meeting room users;
- leisure club users.

Summary

An operator will identify that there exists no one market for hospitality products, rather a range of groups and individuals who, despite utilising similar facilities, will have varying reasons for doing so.

The operator will attempt to identify the general characteristics of such groups, providing products, facilities and services accompanied by the most appropriate marketing mix in an attempt to satisfy this wide variety of needs, requirements and preferences.

This is explained in the sections 'The industry and its products', and 'The approach to marketing by the various sectors' (below).

The industry and its products

In the previous section, the importance of hospitality operators to understand the existence of different market groups or segments, and the effects of the various influences on customer behaviour were identified.

This section will concentrate on what is referred to throughout this book as 'the product' or 'hospitality products', and how hospitality operators utilise marketing techniques to identify the most appropriate mix of products to attract customers. The hospitality industry does not offer one particular product, rather it offers a package of products. Often hospitality services and facilities are not real products in themselves, but a 'bundle' of customer benefits. Hospitality operators tend to utilise styles of marketing and sales different to many product-orientated industries, and so marketing and sales personnel need to have an understanding of such specialist product selling.

WHAT IS A PRODUCT?
'A thing which is made or manufactured.'
Source: *Dictionary of Marketing* by P Collins Publishing, Teddington, Middlesex, 1989.

If you exclude meals or drinks, you can see the hospitality industry offers more than just products. For instance:

- A hotel offers not only accommodation, but also relaxation, security and warmth.
- A fast-food restaurant offers not only hot meals, but also convenience and speed.
- A tourist facility offers cultural interest facts and relaxation opportunities.
- A conference facility may offer not only specialist audio-visual systems, but also opportunities for business and social discussion in appropriate surroundings.
- A holiday facility may offer not only a swimming pool and physical recreation facilities, but also the opportunity to unwind, practise a hobby or just have fun.

Therefore hospitality 'products' are more than just single items produced for sale – they are a mix of products, services, facilities, opportunities and benefits which have to be packaged and promoted in a specialist way. This could be explained further by stating in rather basic terms the following:

- The Savoy Hotel does not sell bedrooms, but status and style.
- The Little Chef does not sell food and drink, but convenience of location.
- McDonalds does not sell hamburgers, but speed of service.
- Center Parcs does not sell holiday accommodation, but the opportunity for relaxation with friends and family.

Obviously, the hospitality industry approaches its planning and marketing and sales along more complex lines. However, if you look at the advertising material of many of these operators, you will quickly identify this aspect of 'benefit' rather than product selling.

WHAT ARE HOSPITALITY PRODUCTS?

Marketing and sales personnel look at hospitality products in a specialist way. They are not concerned in the main with the physical or material composition of the products, rather with the benefits from which customers will derive satisfaction. For many introducing themselves to hospitality marketing and sales, such explanations appear at first confusing: surely a hotel sells accommodation, a restaurant sells food and a licensed premise sells drinks? The following will be useful to explain further this 'benefit' or customer-orientated marketing approach.

THE HOSPITALITY PRODUCT

This is not one single product, such as bedrooms, meals or conference facilities, it is rather a mix of products with added benefits to the customer.

THE CORE PRODUCT

This relates to the fundamental benefit the customer receives, that is, sleep, food and drink, and facilities to satisfy business need. Some hospitality operators do offer a core product concentrating on one particular benefit, for instance, Travel Lodge's core product could be identified as low-cost overnight accommodation.

PRODUCT RANGE

This is a series of products the customer can choose from – Travel Lodge, Granada Lodge, Welcome Break, Quality Inns and Sleep Inns, among others, offer low-cost overnight accommodation, for example; or is a series of differing products from the same group or operator. An example would be a large chain such as Forte Hotels who offer a wide range of accommodation at different places, whilst a single hotel may offer overnight accommodation, business lunches, special weekend breaks, conference and function facilities.

PRODUCT MIX

This is a particular combination of products from a company or unit. For instance, a city centre hotel may offer overnight accommodation for the business traveller, weekend breaks for the tourist, leisure facilities for overnight guests and locals, an á la carte evening restaurant, business lunches, Sunday lunches for families, conference facilities and a bar with a jazz band on certain nights. All are products in their own right, and will attract differing types of customers who will derive different benefits or satisfaction from them. (We will return to this later in the section.)

PRODUCT DIFFERENTIATION

Hospitality operators who offer similar types of products will attempt to differentiate their products from those of their competitors, attempting to identify in the customer's mind some unique features or benefits. This may occur at a fairly basic level, for instance, price, where the operator attempts to increase sales on the better cost value of a particular product. Or it may occur at a much more complex level when advertising and promotion seek to establish a unique position for the product in relation to physiological or psychological factors.

PRODUCT STRATEGY

This is the consideration of the various elements, such as price, design, location, availability and competition, that an operator takes into account when developing a product or product range.

From the above it can be seen that when considering the hospitality product there exists no simple, concise definition to aid the operator, rather a series of considerations which affect the way marketing and sales activity is undertaken.

It is also important to appreciate that while large-scale operators and professional marketing and advertising agencies will use such terms, the hospitality operator will need a more simplified framework to develop and undertake such activities as:

- developing appropriate products;
- planning a marketing and sales strategy; and
- undertaking marketing and sales activities.

A FRAMEWORK FOR HOSPITALITY PRODUCTS — THE MARKETING MIX

In the list of definitions provided above, I referred to a combination of products as the 'product mix', and said that companies often offer a range or mix of products designed to attract different types of customers. Additionally, that there needs to be consideration of the various elements which may act as customer benefits. Marketing personnel refer to this concept as the 'marketing mix' or the four P's (see below).

DEFINITION OF THE MARKETING MIX
The combination of elements which provide for the operator the most appropriate package of benefits required to satisfy identified customer needs.

The marketing mix will identify the most attractive package for the customer, and provide the operator with guidelines of how to achieve increased sales.

This approach is a basic one, and although critics over the years have argued for more sophisticated approaches, it does provide a good, basic marketing framework which busy operators can quickly and readily work within.

THE FOUR P'S

The four P's of the marketing mix are identified as:

- product,
- price,
- place,
- promotion.

Accepting the existence of more complex approaches, this four-element approach forms for many the central focus for all marketing and sales activity. If you look at each element in detail, you will be able to identify the relevance of the market mix concept to maximising sales with the hospitality industry.

THE PRODUCT

In earlier sections of this chapter you learned that the hospitality industry has no one product, rather a range of products which are aimed at attracting different customers at different times and for different reasons. The hospitality product is both a set of primary products, that is, food, drink and accommodation, and a set of secondary products, such as convenience and quality.

Hospitality operators need to:

- Identify the type of product or products to which particular market segments will be attracted.
- Identify and forecast the amount of demand for a particular product, that is, the type of customer and degree of demand.
- Identify whether they can satisfy this product demand, for example, for weekend breaks or conference facilities.
- Identify other elements or characteristics of the demand in order to set a price level that will achieve a profit.

Product identification works at the larger level, for example, when researching the need or market demand for appropriately sited accommodation units for a large leisure facility; and at the lower level, for example, when researching the potential demand for a speciality evening in a hotel's restaurant.

Having identified the product or products the customer may purchase, the operator needs to look in more detail at the packaging of the product, its price, place and promotion to indicate the most appropriate marketing strategy.

THE PRICE

When looking at price it would appear that the marketeer is concentrating on a single, easily defined aspect, that is, the charge to the customer. It is certainly true that the industry attempts to promote and increase sales by utilising this approach. Several hotels, restaurants and travel accommodation units display price banners, for example:

'Only £29.95 per room'
'Three-course lunch at £6.95'
'Bargain priced break'.

If price is the satisfaction element or benefit the customer requires, then this strategy can be deemed to have relevance. However, the actual price or charge to the customer is often not as important as other considerations. Highly priced products may sell more than low-priced products possessing the same characteristics.

The 'price' a customer may pay for making use of a product may include other factors, such as sacrifice, inconvenience, time or organisation.

While market research may have identified the price at which the customer may be attracted, the operator also has to consider other influences on pricing decision making, including set-up costs, such as planning and advertising; operational costs; fixed costs, such as rates and rent; and variable costs, such as food and commodities. A number of costs are controllable or fixed to the element of demand as identified above; some are uncontrollable, such as fluctuations in demand and other agencies increasing their costs.

The pricing considerations will then determine:

- the price band that will best attract purchases; and
- the price to be charged to take into account the related costs and the need for return or profit.

Pricing strategy. The pricing strategy an operator decides upon can be quite varied. While the considerations listed above provide the basis for product pricing, the operator may decide to adapt a particular pricing due to other market considerations.

There are other pricing strategies, and some operators may utilise a variety of pricing strategies.

Having defined the product and possible pricing strategy, the operator then has to consider the third of the four P's, that is, place.

THE PLACE (OR DISTRIBUTION)

This is concerned not just with the physical location of the unit or product, but its accessibility and convenience for the customer. The concept of the 'place' refers to where the product will be physically available, and the process by which customers are made aware and channelled into making a purchase.

Hospitality operators need to:

- Ensure their products are available and that customers can purchase and utilise them.
- Ensure that despite competition the products are readily accessible.

Table 1.1 Types of pricing strategy

Pricing strategy	Objectives	Advantages	Disadvantages	Marketing and sales activity
Low price: market penetration or sales-orientated strategy	Gain entry into new market Capture customers from competitors Increase sales volume Attract customers to sample or test product Attract repeat business	Low price may attract customers to sample a trial product Differentiates operator's product (if of same type) to competitors' products Is appropriate in times of inflation or recession	Possible low customer esteem of product, i.e. low price means low quality Starting with low price makes price rises difficult Larger sales volume needed to return reasonable profits Slow payback of investment	Selling by price Need for aggressive sales activities Need to clearly identify potential demand and profit/costs Product-orientated selling
High price: profit-orientated strategy	Maximisation of profit Rapid payback of investment	High price will equate with high quality worth or value Easier to reduce price when market circumstances allow or enforce Some markets are insensitive to a high-price strategy	Risk that high price will not equate with high quality	Selling or quality worth or benefit Related high costs of promotion and sales
Competition-orientated or multiprice strategy	To match competitors' pricing To obtain share of existing market by comparison selling	Maintains element of differentiation Competes at same level with competitors	Possible need to differentiate products in other ways Differing unit costs may affect real profit margins Differing units may be in different market positions	Need to sell by comparison Need to target activity precisely Marketing will need in the end to differentiate the product from competitors' products

It is important to understand the particular roles aspects of the 'place' play in marketing and sales activity:

- Place – the physical location or availability of a product or range of products.
- Availability – the amount a product is capable of being acquired and utilised.
- Accessibility – the level of ease or difficulty that buyers and potential buyers experience in obtaining the product.
- Channels of distribution – the system of organisation through which products are made available and transferred to customers.

The importance of place and distribution. The hospitality industry is a geographically separated industry with geographically separated markets. Unlike many other industries, the hospitality industry relies on its customers entering its premises to purchase and utilise products. While certain contract or event caterers will take the product to customers, in the main operators require their customers to come to them.

The selection of physical location is important, although some operators utilise remoteness of location and inaccessibility to great effect. The location of a unit is dependent on a variety of factors including:

- accessibility for customers;
- existence of other competitors;
- existence of other units from a group or company;
- costs;
- sites and services available.

The operator will seek to locate the premises where the aspect of physical accessibility (or lack of it) will attract the appropriate level of business.

This factor should also be considered when siting certain facilities within a unit, for instance, the entrance to the hotel bar to attract or dissuade non-resident users. Having identified the best physical location of a unit or facility, the operator then has to consider other aspects of accessibility and availability.

Availability and channels of distribution. A manufacturer of, say, washing machines will identify appropriate distribution and retailing outlets where potential customers can view the product. For the hospitality industry, the product is not so 'tangible', and so operators make use of a variety of specialised activities, agencies and distribution channels in order to create increased awareness of its product range and ease purchasing problems for the customer.

Types of hospitality distribution channels. There exist many barriers in respect of access to potential buyers of hospitality products. While direct selling has positive advantages for the operator, in many situations it will not raise the required levels of awareness and demand. The operator will then turn to intermediaries such as:

- marketing groups, usually made up of independent hotels, restaurants or guest houses;
- travel agents;
- tour operators;
- referral organisations;
- travel companies, for example, airlines and railways;
- tourist boards;
- centralised reservation systems;
- convention or conference booking agencies.

There is a cost element to the utilisation of such intermediaries, either in the form of discount or direct fees. However, by forming partnerships, operators are able to widen the opportunities for sales by creating easier access to information relating to their particular products.

The appropriate selection of intermediaries is an important consideration. the operator will want to ensure that not only is a wider potential 'audience' reached, but also the intermediaries are targeting the most appropriate customer market for the operator. Additionally, due to the number and location of a particular unit, there will be an operator-based intermediary function in selling the company's other units or products.

PROMOTION

Having defined the product or product range, identified the most appropriate pricing strategy and created the physical means by which customers may recognise products and purchase them, the operator needs to define and plan how information related to the product will be communicated and promoted to potential customers.

While promotion is described in some detail in Chapter 4, it is important to identify the basis on which promotion is made use of by the industry.

The importance of promotion. Hospitality operators need to communicate effectively and positively with both potential and existing customers. Positive promotional methods are utilised to:

- increase customer awareness of products;
- create favourable and appropriate demand for products;
- maintain demand for products;
- raise awareness for a particular company or product;
- create a market or brand position for a particular company.

While promotion can be simply translated as advertising or promotional messages, the manner in which the communication is delivered and received is much more complex. A detailed study of communication theory is outside the scope of this text.

Sales personnel often have an understanding of the problems associated with effective communication and promotion, and by experience can identify the best methods for communicating and promoting particular products. They are experienced in utilising the set of communication tools or mix of promotional activities that will achieve identified sales objectives. Such tools include the use of all, or some, of the following:

- advertising (in all its forms);
- direct selling or direct mail;
- merchandising;
- public relations;
- sales promotions;
- sponsorship;
- the use of computer technology;
- telephone selling.

Whatever the method or tool utilised, the aim is to increase sales by enhancing the product with selling messages. Having identified the market, the product and the price, the operator can usually identify fairly accurately the most appropriate type of communication or promotional message.

CONCLUSION

The industry has a special problem related to its products in that many are not tangible and, therefore, require a special approach to marketing and sales planning and activity. Due to the wide variety of its products which are designed to provide for a physically separated 'audience', the industry has to seek positive and cost-effective ways of creating accessibility for its goods, services and facilities. The utilisation of the correct marketing mix can assist the operator in creating, maintaining and increasing profitable sales.

The next section will look at the outline differences in approach to marketing and sales by the various sectors within the industry.

THE APPROACH TO MARKETING BY THE VARIOUS SECTORS

In 'The hospitality industry' (above), I outlined a simplified structure which identified the two main areas of the industry: the commercial sector and the welfare sector. Additionally, the main differences in general marketing approaches were identified. The sections, 'Markets and customers' and 'The industry and its products' (above) looked in detail at the range of specialist considerations operators evaluate in respect of marketing activity.

Having recognised these structural and operational differences, it is now important to study in more detail the way various types of operators approach and undertake marketing and sales activity. Certain common activities exist, including the importance of identifying customer needs and level of demand. Marketing and sales methods or such processes as advertising, direct mail, selling skills, public relations and in-house promotion and sales, are all used by the majority of operators. What differs is the range and scope of such activity.

Operators will want to utilise activities that directly relate to their style of operation, the product range and the types of market and customer.

THE LICENSED TRADE

This sector is dominated by public houses owned and operated by the major brewery companies, but also includes growing numbers of theme bars, night-clubs and public houses and inns owned by independent operators.

The licensed trade has undergone considerable structural changes over the past few years, with many of the larger operators shedding units due to pressure from the government to reduce the size of brewery holdings and widen the choice for the consumer. In addition the nature of the market has changed, too.

Customer demand for more traditional public houses has declined, which has not been assisted by the excessive number of premises attempting to serve an increasingly sophisticated market. The decline in wet sales, due in part to stricter drink-driving laws, has been partly offset by the rise in demand for food and other types of services.

Units will attempt to target particular segments of the market which can be generally grouped as follows:

- the young adult market;
- families and couples;
- local workers;
- tourists.

Some houses may attract elements of each market, while some concentrate on providing products and services specifically aimed at a particular market. Public houses may also follow a theme, for instance, folk music.

The public house owner, tenant or manager will look at activities designed to attract and maintain demand. This will be assisted by the style and range of facilities. Licensed premises, such as private clubs, working men's clubs and night-clubs, also operate in this way.

The larger operators and bodies, such as the Brewers Society, carry out research on the market in an attempt to identify general trends. Over the past few years, the sector has seen increasing demand from families and identified the need to provide for growing numbers of female customers. Additionally, a considerable number of bars has been opened, designed to attract the young adult market with appropriate furniture and fixtures, music and videos.

The change in the licensing laws in England allowing more flexible opening hours has followed similar legislation in Scotland. This change has also affected customers' buying behaviour.

GENERAL CHARACTERISTICS OF MARKETING AND SALES ACTIVITY

- Facilities have been altered in an attempt to satisfy a rapidly changing and sophisticated market.
- In general, units attempt to satisfy a particular type of customer, and many of the larger operators attempt to create units to serve segmented market groups.
- Marketing is an activity usually undertaken by the larger brewery companies, while smaller operators concentrate on more local activity.
- Promotional and sales activities are usually centred on providing for more local audiences.
- Advertising is a fairly minimal activity, with an emphasis on certain events, refurbishment and special offers.
- Merchandising is concentrated on the promotion and sale of certain beverages.
- Some premises will make use of exterior wall advertising to promote food or facilities.
- Some units will utilise image creators, such as window boxes, to reinforce their position as 'olde worlde' premises.
- A considerable number of units undertake little or no marketing and sales activity.

PREDICTIONS FOR THE FUTURE

- While some new units will attract a considerable number of customers, the general trend is for a reduction in the overall number of units.
- Operators will increase promotional and sales activity in an attempt to win back customers.
- Customer care standards will improve, especially with regards to markets for older age-groups.
- Licensed premises, especially public houses, will attempt to satisfy markets by an increasing level of facilities.

'Effective marketing is of vital importance to our company and the individual licensees due to increased competition and the change in customer demand. Licensed premises differ greatly to the hotel sector, although many of our houses offer accommodation and operate high-quality food provision similar to hotel operators.

In developing marketing practice, we involve the licensee in specific training programmes, which include market research, identifying potential markets, food and drink merchandising, and promotional activities and customer-care techniques. Due to the nature of the business, advertising, direct mail and promotional activities are not centrally co-ordinated and, in many respects, are inappropriate for such an organisation. I would estimate that our main strategy in the future would be to effectively market and sell food provision and this requires particular strategies aimed at local markets.'

Source: Richard Ward, Area Manager and Catering Advisor for Wards, a Sheffield-based brewery with over 200 licensed premises within Yorkshire and Humberside.

The hotel sector

The problem with this sector is its diversity. It is not realistic to equate a luxury, five-star London hotel with a small, 12-bedroomed hotel in a quiet rural area. While the sector is seen by many to be dominated by the larger operators, that is, Fortes, Swallow, The Hilton Group, Holiday Inns and Queens Moat Houses, the predominance is on the small independent operator.

In general terms, the hotel market is fairly saturated, a situation which has not been helped by the reduction in demand due to economic factors.

Lodge hotels

While several companies operate lodge hotels, it is interesting to look in some detail at one particular company, Campanile Hotels (UK) Ltd.

This French owned company currently operates 12 lodge-type hotels throughout the UK. With steady but progressive development plans, the company has a particular approach to marketing and sales activity. Unlike other operators in this sector, Campanile conducts marketing activity mainly on a local basis. Each hotel is managed by a married couple with considerable freedom to develop and maintain local business. John Bevan is the company's UK Sales and Marketing Director. 'Our aim is to establish a

(continued)

strong brand image for our hotels based on value for money facilities with friendly family service.'

The management couple are provided with an annual budget for marketing and sales activity, and encouraged and assisted to develop local contacts. Membership of the local Chamber of Commerce, tourist agencies, Hotels' Association and other bodies is seen as vitally important in 'integrating' the hotel into the local community.

Campanile's main activities are targeted at the local business market, and the hotel managers make use of a variety of methods to raise awareness of the unit and develop profitable business.

Local mailshots are undertaken prior, during and after a unit officially opens. Such mailshots will often include up to 40,000 items, usually distributed via a local newspaper.

Cocktail lunches are held for local secretaries, with an average invitation list of over 300. Bevan: 'We usually attract a reasonable number of secretaries who are greeted by hotel staff, provided with a tour of rooms, the restaurant and conference facilities and a buffet lunch. The aim is to encourage the secretaries to view and sample the quality of our provision, and then consider utilising the hotel for their accommodation needs.'

While the bedrooms provide the bulk of revenue, marketing and sales activity targeted at potential users of the restaurant is also undertaken. Mailing lists are either provided by the company or purchased, and mailshot numbers could exceed 40,000. Local advertising is also undertaken on a regular basis – proving the old adage that repetition of advertisements can work.

Alongside this localised activity are more national actions. The company does not as yet advertise nationally. As Bevan explains: 'For the cost of national advertising we can employ a tele-sales company to make our 10,000 targeted tele-sales calls. In a test run conducted recently, the results were extremely favourable with 288 enquiries out of 500 calls.'

The company also recognises the importance of public relations and employs a PR agency to handle national events and press relations. The unit managers are also encouraged to utilise PR to improve local awareness of their hotel.

Due to its links with its parent company, Campanile attends various national and international travel trade fairs, where activities are concentrated on tour operators and agencies.

Bevan: 'It's true that we need a particular approach to our marketing and sales activity. Actions must concentrate on creating increased customer awareness and a strong brand image linked to the local business market. With the expansion of the number of units, the emphasis of our marketing will perhaps alter. The market for lower cost, lodge-type accommodation certainly exists, especially as companies are looking more closely at the costs of the traditional two- to three-star hotel operation.'

THE TRADITIONAL HOTEL SECTOR

This sector of the industry has realised considerable growth over the past few decades. Increasing numbers of two- to three-star hotels have been opened, and some of the larger companies have attempted to differentiate their hotel product range. For companies with multiple sites, the approach to marketing and sales has become increasingly sophisticated.

GENERAL CHARACTERISTICS OF MARKETING AND SALES ACTIVITY

- National advertising via various media is increasing; in early 1992, Fortes was the first company to try out national television advertising, an action others may follow.
- The larger companies either operate their own central reservations system, and/or link with other agents to increase appropriate channels of distribution.
- The capture of marketing information is seen as increasingly important, and companies utilise their own data, tele-research and purchased market information in an attempt to identify customer needs more accurately.
- Many operators within this sector are moving to establish stronger brand images in an attempt to create improved brand awareness and loyalty.
- The marketing and sales function is operated on a national, regional and unit level, with increased emphasis on targeting activity at developing markets.
- There exists a trend towards improving customer care and in-house promotion and sales as overall demand reduces.

PREDICTIONS FOR THE FUTURE

- The trend will be towards a wider business mix with less reliance on the declining business or commercial market.
- While price reductions will slow down in general, the attitude towards pricing will become more customer sensitive.
- Increased emphasis will be placed on developing staff skills in customer care in order to maintain business and increasing sales volume.

THE INDEPENDENT HOTEL

Independent hotel operators form a large part of the hotel sector and, faced with problems similar to the larger hotel chains with the additional factor of a weaker market position, have particular challenges in respect of marketing and sales.

Lacking the sophisticated channels of distribution traditionally only available to the larger operator, the independent operator relies on a more personalised strategy and approach.

GENERAL CHARACTERISTICS OF MARKETING AND SALES ACTIVITY

- Marketing is often a fairly low-level activity with emphasis being on promotion and sales activities and actions.
- The customer base is often fairly specialised and depends considerably on the strength of the hotel's position in the local market.
- Advertising is usually only through guides or local media.
- Channels of distribution tend to be tourist board guides and marketing consortiums.
- Activities, such as public relations, publicity and sales, are often undertaken by the manager or owner, who, faced with other operational management functions, will be unable to spend the appropriate amount of time on such activities.

PREDICTIONS FOR THE FUTURE

- Operators will increase their use of technology to capture and utilise customer data.
- Increasing numbers will join marketing consortiums.
- Emphasis will be on increasing the local market and expanding a variety of other worthwhile market groups which are, at present, under represented.
- Larger numbers of operators will seek to expand their facilities, especially in relation to leisure.

RESTAURANT CHAINS

Chains such as Berni, Harvester, Pizzahut, and Cavalier, operate on a strong brand image. With careful selection of sites, they produce a highly selected menu designed to attract families, couples and young adults. The emphasis is on bright, colourful menus with items individually priced – a version of fixed-fare à la carte provision. The accent is on quick and informal service in appropriate surroundings with increased hours of opening.

GENERAL CHARACTERISTICS OF MARKETING AND SALES ACTIVITY

- Activities centre on establishing a strong brand image helped by the number of units available.
- Advertising is usually only local, although some of the pizza chains do undertake national TV advertising.
- Sales material is bright, colourful, some would say 'brash' and highly targeted at price/quality/convenience factors.
- Little or no attempt is made to capture customer data.
- In-house merchandising activities are considerable with a steady flow of promotions and price reductions.

PREDICTIONS FOR THE FUTURE

- There will be a continued growth in types of chain speciality restaurants, including Mexican, American and Asian restaurants.
- Their main product, that is, food and beverages, will alter as demand declines due to customer 'menu fatigue'.
- Operators will expect unit staff to be more involved with the local community in an attempt to personalise their activities.
- Numbers of older staff will increase as operators realise the contribution such staff can make in terms of customer care, increased sales volume and unit (rather than brand) loyalty.

SPECIALIST TOURIST ATTRACTIONS

For operators who do not fit into the general category of hotels and restaurants, the approach to marketing and sales activity will be based upon the type of operation and market.

One unique specialist tourist 'operation' is Granada Studio Tours in Manchester, which encompasses a variety of products, services and facilities around the theme of television and film.

Opened in 1988, it is now one of the UK's leading tourist attractions and has won several awards including the British Tourist Authority 'Tourism Marketing Award' and, in 1991, the 'Overall Leisure Attraction Award'. Over two and a half million visitors had utilised the facilities up to the beginning of 1992. The mix of facilities include backstage tours, restaurants, catering and merchandising units, themed areas, conference, function and event facilities, film studios, TV sets (including a full House of Commons set) and, due for opening late 1992, a hotel designed to complement the above facilities.

With such a range of provision, the approach to marketing and sales has to be highly specialised, with ongoing analysis of actual business and investigation into other potential markets.

The marketing and sales activity is undertaken by a specialist team who have a positive and systematic approach. The effective investigation, planning and implementation of activity form a vital element of the overall marketing strategy.

Such activity not only has to market, promote and sell the general operation, but also consider cost effective methods for the many specialist facilities that may attract customers in their own right.

Targeted marketing and sales activity is of increasing importance. The marketing and sales team utilises sophisticated mailshots to target corporate businesses, travel and tour operators, educational parties, groups and individual visitors. Tele-research and sales is conducted on an ongoing basis,

(continued)

---

coupled with detailed analysis of past business. With customer numbers in 1992 estimated to be in excess of 700,000, such analysis will provide important marketing information. Not only would such data identify the type of customer, but also more importantly the source or origin of the business. This is especially important in respect of a growing overseas market.

Attendance at major tourism conferences and exhibitions, membership of various trade associations and joint initiatives with conference agents and tour operators assist the development of business and increase distribution channels. Targeted advertising is backed up by a range of specialist, high-quality brochures, and regular invitations are sent out to prospective clients for product-sampling visits.

Ian Lamaison, of the Corporate Sales Department at Granada Studios Tours, recognises the challenge in marketing and selling such a unique facility: 'We have no particular secrets – our activities concentrate on ongoing analysis of customer needs and involves basic hard work targeted at providing quality facilities.'

With the opportunity for visitors to view multi-media presentations, visit Coronation Street, act as the Prime Minister in a live debate, gain information about the industry of cinema and television and take part in product launches, company conferences and functions, the approach to marketing and sales is highly specialised. Such specialisation provides a particular challenge for operators with a highly sophisticated product mix.

SECTION SUMMARY

This section has attempted to provide an overview of the various approaches to general marketing and sales activity. This is only a 'snapshot', and the number of examples could have been increased, for instance, to include exclusive country house hotels, five-star luxury hotels, fast-food operators, contract and event caterers and specialist leisure facilities.

What is important is the recognition that the various sectors will have different approaches to activity, especially in regard to promotion and sales. All operators will want to identify clearly the characteristics and needs of their markets, and provide staff with the appropriate mechanisms and tools to achieve the aim of maintaining and developing business.

The role of staff in such activities is of considerable importance, and this aspect is dealt with in the final section of this chapter: 'The marketing and sales function'.

THE MARKETING AND SALES FUNCTION

This section will concentrate on how the marketing and sales function is organised within the hospitality industry. It will identify the role and function of marketing and sales departments, and explore in brief the use of external agencies.

Many of the textbooks on marketing do not look in sufficient detail at these aspects which, perhaps, has led in part to the old-fashioned idea that hospitality marketing and sales personnel lead a rather 'glamorous' existence.

Additionally, for many individuals working in the industry, the function and role of such departments has been seen as perhaps, at best, complementary to the work and activities they undertake. The hospitality industry is about team work, and all who work positively and effectively contribute to its success. The majority of marketing and sales personnel and individuals who really understand the importance of sales and marketing will point out that all individuals within a unit or company are sales persons.

THE ORGANISATION OF THE MARKETING AND SALES FUNCTION

The way in which this function is organised and utilised by the industry differs from company to company. It will depend on a variety of factors including:

- the size and style of the company or unit;
- geographical spread;
- the market position of the company;
- the degree of autonomy of unit managers;
- costs;
- the method of distribution (see 'The industry and its products' (above));
- the degree of branding and commonality of style;
- the use of external marketing agencies.

What perhaps is common is the particular specialist role that marketing and sales personnel have, be they solely undertaking this responsibility or in addition to other roles within the company or unit.

THE NATIONAL MARKETING DEPARTMENT

The role of this department is to undertake the overall planning, organisation and actioning of the company's corporate marketing objectives. It would initiate national advertising and promotional campaigns, conduct research, create national partnerships with other distributors, control and direct regional and unit personnel, and provide consolidated reports to the group's managing director or board.

For operators with strongly branded units, for example, Harvester

Restaurants, Little Chef and Pizzahut, this national or head office facility may exist with little need for regional or unit sales personnel. The advantages are cost reduction, commonality of approach, and reduction in overall response time to alterations in market demand.

However, when units are not strongly branded, and they rely on a more personalised approach to marketing and sales, the decentralisation of this function becomes increasingly important.

REGIONAL MARKETING AND SALES DEPARTMENTS

Swallow Hotels operates several regional sales offices or departments. Their role is complementary to the national office and, while utilising centralised facilities, concentrates on a small group of hotels developing more personal contact with potential clients and hotel staff.

Swallow Hotels operates 33 hotels throughout the country. This highly successful chain, sixth in the classification of the UK's hotel groups, has several regional offices.

Irene Holdsworth, Northern Regional Sales Manager, identified the role of sales executives as: 'To win business for the hotels within the group. The role can be further broken down into certain key areas:

- Contacting potential clients to identify their potential needs.
- Establishing details of projected business.
- Identifying decision makers in companies and organisations.

The focus must be on action to turn potential business into actual business.'

A regional office is extremely busy where research of media, publications, telephone selling and personal sales calls form part of an overall marketing plan.

Holdsworth: 'In addition to developing contacts and winning business for the organisation, the sales office undertakes other vital functions, including the management of sales, data capture, analysis of business, training staff in sales skills, sales audits of units and developing positive sales action plans.'

Regional sales offices can be very proactive in conducting research on companies and groups, in identifying local market information and establishing and maintaining personal contact with potential and regular customers. They can build up more detailed data on potential customers and past users. Their separation from the actual unit has advantages, in that by being separated they can often blitz particular markets over a short, intensive period. They can provide unit managers with information related to both other units and competitors, and advise unit staff on positive marketing and sales methods.

Additionally, they may deal with regional tour operators, booking companies and travel agents, arranging regional discounts or packages which an individual unit may not be able to satisfy. However, due to their physical separation from regionally spread units, they often cannot offer the more personalised service provided by a unit marketing and sales office.

THE UNIT MARKETING AND SALES DEPARTMENT

Whether the unit is part of a group or is independent, unit marketing and sales personnel perform a vital function. While in larger units there may be several staff with separate responsibilities for group accommodation, banqueting and conference sales or corporate sales, all the personnel provide a personalized approach to sales.

> 'While one can recognise the advantage of national and regional sales teams, individual units also benefit from operating an effective sales team. Sales staff can concentrate on the specific unit creating a more personal relationship with customers.'
> Source: Peter Ord, Corporate Sales Manager, Forte's Cumberland Hotel, London.

Unit personnel are able to obtain information on the unit's potential and existing customers. They identify fairly rapidly local business trends and sales opportunities by researching the local market and immediate competitors. Most importantly, they can deal face to face with potential customers and follow through bookings positively with users.

Their role is primarily to identify potential business for the unit and develop profitable sales. Additionally, it may be that they plan and undertake unit sales and promotional activities without the assistance of external agencies.

Developing a Sales Support Team

Due to their specialism, they may also undertake the direct training of unit personnel in marketing and sales and positive customer-care techniques.

For a small operator with a limited number of staff, the responsibility for this function may fall to the unit manager or proprietor. The time available for such activities may be limited, yet its importance remains.

Summary

Whether the operator uses a centralised marketing and sales function, regional or unit-based function (or a mixture of all three), there exists definite advantages in some separation of the responsibility from the operational side of the organisation. However, increasingly, this function is seen as one best carried our within a unit, with, if possible, additional company or external assistance.

The use of external marketing and sales agencies

In 'The industry and its products' (above), we saw how operators will often use additional channels of distribution to raise customer awareness and increase the accessibility of products. Operators will also utilise specialist external agencies for all or part of their marketing and sales activity. Such agencies could include:

Advertising agencies. Support could include the identification of appropriate campaigns, the design of advertising material, the purchase of advertising space and evaluation of responses. In addition, they can provide information to the operator on how best to reach particular market targets.

Public relations agencies. Support could include the preparation, organisation and management of PR events, liaison with the media, and the preparation of product launches and publicity material.

Sales representations and agencies. Support could include acting as an additional distribution channel for the operator in particular areas, sales calls and presentations, the identification of potential clients, the setting up of sales calls for operators, and the operating of sales stands at exhibitions.

Direct mail companies. Support could include the design and print of direct mail material, the identification of target groups or individuals for campaigns, processing, distribution and response handling.

Marketing consultants. Support could include the analysis of the operator's business, the identification of potential markets, advice on emerging products and markets, staff training and the preparation of marketing and sales plans.

'Consultants provide the hotel proprietor and manager with an honest and objective assessment of their business. The experience of the industry and the specialist knowledge built up over many years give the consultant an understanding of how to help improve the profitability of a business. A hotel marketing consultant can provide advice on how to: improve the product, plan the future development of the business and develop sales campaigns.

'Most hoteliers still think that marketing is the same as advertising and they rarely consider other elements in the marketing mix when planning their promotional campaigns, because the simple basics have been forgotten. The marketing consultant will ensure that the business is satisfying the customers' needs; that prices and the competition have been carefully considered; and then help plan a cost effective campaign using the hotel's "unique selling points".

'However, when employing a consultant, care must be taken to ensure that the consultant does have the requisite industry experience coupled with a good track record in consultancy. It is important to take up references from some of the consultant's previous clients.'
Source: David Bowie, Consultant.

There also exist other types of agencies which specialise in market research, design and copywriting.

There is a cost factor to be considered, and operators may lack the specialist knowledge or experience, or the time to undertake particular activities. Additionally, they may decide that by employing an external agent or company, they will reduce their own costs.

External agencies or companies will provide specialist assistance for any size of operator, and may be utilised to back up marketing and sales activity undertaken by operator's specialist personnel.

GOVERNMENT ASSISTANCE

There are a variety of government sponsored schemes available through the Department of Trade and Industry, concerned with marketing consultancy and initiatives.

For smaller hospitality units, such as the hotels identified above, the financial outlay on marketing and sales personnel would be inappropriate. In periods of high business turnover, such operators may conduct fairly low level marketing and sales activity, relying on personal recommendations and small-scale advertising to maintain business. However, when demand reduces and competition increases, as was apparent in the early 1990s, such operators can face serious problems. The schemes sponsored by the government may provide part solutions to such situations. The Enterprise Initiative assists organisations with marketing and production development Positive examples of such schemes provide both technical and financial assistance to the industry.

JOB PROFILES

Having explored the various ways of organising the marketing and sales function and identified the external agencies which the hospitality industry utilises, it is important to look briefly at marketing and sales personnel and the type of skills and knowledge they require.

JOB PROFILE

JOB TITLE	Sales & Marketing Manager
REPORTS TO	General Manager
RESPONSIBLE FOR:	Sales & Marketing

PRINCIPAL RESPONSIBILITIES

Management & organisation of sales & marketing department

Development of sales plan and strategies to maximise membership potential

Conduct personal sales of membership

Development & presentation of the Corporate membership package

Development & improvement of internal marketing of club

Responsibility for obtaining PR in defined market places

Preparation of weekly, monthly & annual sales projections & reports

Improvement of Club's profile within the Leisure industry

Production of the Club's monthly newsletter

Development & sale of Event sponsorship, assistance with the planning & execution of the events

Management & development of Sales/Marketing Assistant

Duty Management (operations) responsibility

Keeping up-to-date statistics of Club's competition

Maintaining an awareness of trends within the Leisure industry

---

Fig. 1.5

JOB PROFILE (ABOVE) AND CANDIDATE PROFILE (TOP RIGHT)

Fig. 1.6

(BOTTOM RIGHT AND PAGE 48) A RANGE OF ADVERTISEMENTS FOR THE POST OF SALES MANAGER

CANDIDATE PROFILE

Preferably degree educated – plus 3–4 years experience in a Sales/Marketing role, preferably in private sector Leisure.

Self-motivated, pro-active and flexible.

Must have a strong determination to succeed despite possible setback.

Must have excellent communication skills – both verbal and presentation – and have an ability to communicate with people of all levels and type.

Must understand the concept of a quality service and demonstrate experience in that type of environment.

Basic management skills required.

Operations management (D.M.) an advantage.

Must have worked in a competitive and commercial environment.

Must be able to develop sales strategies and campaigns and convert into memberships.

Must be able to develop a marketing strategy.

Must possess inter-personal and person-management skills.

SALES CONSULTANTS
South East & West Midlands
Package to £40K + Car + Benefits

ABM Catering is the contract catering specialist within the Lindley Group of Companies, who despite the recession was able to treble its client base in the year 1991/1992.

This sustainable growth record has been established on our philosophy of providing clients with a quality led, responsive and flexible service which is financially beyond reproach.

We are now seeking like minded individuals to maintain this philosophy and drive forward our ambitious expansion programme in 1992/93 and beyond.

You will need to be able to demonstrate a sound track record in the gaining of new business in the contract catering market and be capable of working on your own initiative.

If you feel you are able to meet this challenge and wish to develop your career with a dynamic, forward thinking organisation, please send your C.V. to:–

John Duffield, Managing Director,
ABM Catering Limited,
43 High Street, Addlestone,
Surrey KT15 1TU

SVCR22-004*

Harrington Hall

SALES MANAGER

A Sales Manager is now required for Kensington's newest 4 Star Deluxe Hotel, the 200 bedroomed Harrington Hall Hotel, which is due to open in April 1993.

As Sales Manager you will be required to set up the sales office, contracting with travel, corporate and conference clientele, advertising, marketing, and preparing for the opening.

The successful candidate will probaly be aged between 25 to 40, ideally with a minimum of 3 years experience in the hotel industry, and particularly in London. You will have a sound technical knowledge of the business and will have a proven track record of success in obtaining new business. Commercial acumen, self motivation, good organisation, excellent communication and social skills are needed in this interesting and challenging position.

Applications in writing with current C.V. and photograph to:

Mr D. Patterson
Roland House
121 Old Brompton Road
London SW7 3RX

MVCL18/968

Fig. 1.6 (CONTINUED)

HOSPITALITY MARKETING AND SALES PERSONNEL

The main role and responsibilities of marketing and sales personnel were identified above. An appreciation of their personal attributes and skills will provide a useful background to the importance of positive customer care which is the benchmark all operators strive to achieve.

> 'The role of sales staff is to identify potential customers and sell the hotel and its benefits positively. By building up professional relationships with clients, the sales person creates the right link between the hotel and these clients.'
> Source: Peter Ord, Corporate Sales Manager, Forte's Cumberland Hotel, London.

PERSONAL SKILLS AND ATTRIBUTES

Marketing and sales in the hospitality industry is a specialist art due to its emphasis on personal or face-to-face selling, which requires relevant skills and attributes.

The sales individual should possess:

- excellent communication and presentation skills;
- inter-personal and personnel management skills;
- the ability to negotiate positively with potential and existing customers;
- the determination to succeed despite possible setbacks;
- organisational skills;

and the appropriate attitude towards the marketing and sales function, in that they possess knowledge and commitment of the product they are promoting. Successful marketing and sales personnel will attempt to be sympathetic to the needs of a client, treating each potential customer as special.

Such an approach provides the customer with the correct image of the operator, that is, professional, interested in clients and their needs, and caring, which creates customer confidence.

Such skills and attributes come easy to some individuals. However, such personal characteristics must be backed up with knowledge of the goods, services and facilities available – what is often referred to as 'product knowledge'.

PRODUCT KNOWLEDGE

For individuals concerned with marketing and sales or regular customer contact, product knowledge is of vital importance. Whether the individual is selling to corporate clients, tour operators, individuals or in direct contact with customers within a restaurant or bar, knowledge of the range of products available, their price, quality, availability, content and related benefits, forms the basis for proactive and effective selling.

The aim is to provide services or products which match or exceed the customer expectations. The knowledge of the complete product range will assist the sales person in this positive matching process. This aspect is dealt with in more detail in Chapter 5.

CONCLUSION

Marketing and sales departments and related personnel perform a vital function for their respective organisations. The operator should have carefully analysed the market potential and identified customer needs. The operator will then identify particular goals and objectives in relation to the business; it falls to the marketing and sales department or individual to action these objectives into positive activities and outcomes.

The use of external agencies will often assist the operator in achieving specific goals. However, in the end effective marketing and sales relies on people, with the appropriate skills and attributes matched to appropriate products.

CHAPTER REVIEW

This chapter is designed to introduce readers to aspects of the hospitality industry related to the marketing and sales function. It is important to have an understanding of the industry and the position various elements of it hold in the market place. The increasing relevance of marketing and sales activity was explained, and definitions provided on the industry, its markets, customers and products.

In the increasingly competitive market of the 1990s, the need for operators to undertake marketing and sales activities that are cost effective and relate directly to the style of operation, range of products, services, facilities and customers can be easily identified.

Hospitality operators require increased understanding of all the factors that affect or will affect their businesses. Analysis of both existing and potential markets and proactive methods designed to attract, maintain and develop profitable and appropriate business is a key element in today's industry.

The analysis of markets will provide the operator with relevant indicators for decision making. While decisions may be made at board, director or owner level, it is the role of marketing and sales personnel to develop effective actions and positive outcomes. The specialist role of such staff is increasingly seen of importance to the survival of the business, as too is the involvement of all staff in marketing and sales activity.

Chapter 2 will detail the considerations required to 'set' a unit, business or company correctly for targeting markets effectively.

KEY POINTS

- The hospitality industry is extremely diverse, and recognition should be made of the varying factors that have affected its growth and development over the past few decades.
- Despite job losses and sector contraction in the early 1990s, the industry is forecasted to continue expanding, with skills shortages being one of the biggest constraints on its development.
- While it is possible to group various types of hospitality businesses into certain classifications, the important factor is to identify the type of customers and markets companies attempt to satisfy.
- The majority of marketing and sales activities nowadays are considered to be consumer orientated, although there are elements of product-orientated

marketing remaining, and aspects of social-orientated marketing developing.

- Marketing is the management process for identifying and satisfying customer needs profitably. While of growing importance, it is only one element in a range of operational activities.
- The industry attempts to serve increasingly diverse, competitive and sophisticated markets.
- Operators should understand the characteristics of the markets they attempt to serve.
- While the industry offers a variety of products they are less tangible than in other industries and require specialist approaches to marketing and sales

- A common way of looking at marketing is known as the marketing mix or four P's – product, price, promotion and place. Some would argue that you could add a fifth 'P', that of people – referring to both employees and customers.
- While certain marketing and sales activities will be common across the industry, operators need to utilise activities that directly relate to their style of operation, product range and type(s) of market and customer.
- The role of marketing and sales personnel is an increasingly specialised one, which requires particular skills, knowledge and expertise.

QUESTIONS

- Explain the relevance of the title 'hospitality' for the hotel, catering and licensed trade.
- Discuss the increasing importance of effective marketing and sales activity to the survival of hospitality businesses.
- Identify the particular markets the hospitality industry serves with reference to the varying characteristics or buying behaviour of each market.
- Explain the need for operators to understand their existing and potential markets in terms of maintaining and developing appropriate business.
- Describe the main differences in approach to marketing and sales between at least two different sectors of the industry.
- Identify the main marketing strategies and activities a country house hotel would undertake.
- Identify and discuss the factors that have affected the level and type of customer demand for hospitality products in the late 1980s and early 1990s.
- List the personal attributes required for marketing and sales personnel.

CHAPTER TWO

MARKETING PLANNING AND STRATEGY

INTRODUCTION

Throughout this book, illustrations are provided identifying sales and marketing methods and activities designed to improve a unit's or company's business performance. Similar to all business activities, careful planning with identified aims and objectives is a key component of hospitality management.

Knowledge and understanding of both internal and external factors that affect, or will affect the business in the future are requirements of a successfully planned marketing campaign.

Hospitality operators seek to identify strategies that will assist the development, performance and profitability of their units. Having identified a particular strategy, it is the role of planners and planning to achieve success.

While detailed planning is seen by many operators as the best approach, it must also be recognised that many highly successful companies keep planning to a minimum, relying on their knowledge of the industry and skills of staff involved.

Pru Leith, owner of the famous Leith's School of Food and Wine, restaurants, contract caterers and other successful catering businesses, operates in this way. With a turnover of millions, sales and marketing activity is planned through informal regular meetings between the directors of the various businesses. At these meetings, tasks and targets are discussed, reviews taken of business and actions identified.

'We highlight the important tasks and identify them in fairly simple terms. Our sales and marketing activities are action driven and not a result of complicated and costly planning.'

Leith sees no real difference between sales and marketing: 'It is an activity all staff should be involved in and is concerned with customer care and encouraging average spend per head. Sales and marketing activities should be costed like all parts of the business.'

This chapter concentrates on the basic principles and practices of planning, especially in connection with sales and marketing activity. It highlights the importance of planning and explains the concepts of market segmentation and mix, the product life cycle and branding, with a discussion on the importance of the evaluation of results.

It should be remembered that the planning of sales and marketing activity should be integrated into the company or unit's overall planning if it is to be successful.

LEARNING OBJECTIVES

By the end of this chapter you should be able to:

- Identify the main benefits of effective planning.
- Describe the basic planning process in relation to sales and marketing activity.
- Explain the basic concepts of marketing positioning and segmentation.
- Outline the basic principle of the product life cycle and elements of each stage of the cycle that will affect sales and marketing activity.
- List the advantages of branding to large organisations.
- Describe basic methods of evaluating the results of sales and marketing activities.

THE PLANNING PROCESS

The process of planning is dependent upon a variety of factors, such as:

- the nature and style of the business;
- the scale and scope of the proposed activity;
- external factors, including economic climate; and
- internal factors, including management skills.

It will also be dependent upon identified strategic aims, which will vary from operator to operator. For a large group, planning may concentrate on the achievement of a variety of objectives encompassing strategies to improve market share in a particular sector, retain the appropriate volume of business by reducing rates, or to maximise sales volume by increasing average spend per head. For a small operator, planning may concentrate on specific targets, such as increasing the volume of weekend-break visitors in particular periods, or maintaining local customer loyalty by providing appropriate incentives.

This section is not concerned with major corporate strategic planning, rather with the basic considerations and processes required to produce effective sales and marketing plans. In its most basic form, marketing planning is concerned with three simple stages. These stages are often best outlined in the form of three key questions:

- Where is the business now?
- Where does the business need to be in the future?
- How is this to be achieved?

By conducting analysis of internal and external factors affecting the first two stages, the hospitality operator is able to design and implement an appropriate marketing plan. We shall now look at the activities that are involved in each stage.

WHERE IS THE BUSINESS NOW?

This is the most fundamental stage in the planning process. It commonly involves the hospitality operator conducting a detailed analysis of its particular business. The depth of such a review is dependent upon how knowledgeable the operator is on both the business and the environment in which it operates. The operator could be involved in analysis of:

- the present level and type of business;
- the business environment;
- competitors;
- existing strengths and weaknesses of the business;
- potential opportunities and threats.

This stage concentrates on analysing data concerned with past business performance and potential market change and opportunities. It involves the operator in looking both *inwardly* and *outwardly* at the business.

If appropriate information on how the business is performing has been obtained then the operator is able to conduct a 'health' check or audit. This check is often referred to as a SWOT analysis.

SWOT ANALYSIS
The health check may be carried out by looking at the

- Strengths,
- Weaknesses,
- Opportunities, and
- Threats,

that a business possesses. Such an analysis will enable the operator to obtain a clearer picture of where a business is, where it should develop and what may restrict this development.

Analysing business strengths

Every business will have particular strengths. These could range from existing market share, product and facility quality, and low-operating costs to good location, sole-supplier status and management and staff skills. The operator is then concerned with identifying clearly the positive side of the business. Understanding not only what profitable business exists, but also how this business is generated provides the operator with sound planning information.

Analysing business weaknesses

It will be an extremely lucky operator whose business has no weaknesses. These could range from a poor market position, insufficient investment capital, poor product range, to a decline in the main customer base, a poor location and lack of appropriate staff skills. The details analysis of existing weaknesses is just as important as the identification of business strengths. The reason behind the weaknesses must be analysed in an attempt to identify whether corrective action is possible.

Analysing business opportunities

Markets change constantly, although the change may be rapid over a short period of time or slow where consumer behaviour is altering to a variety of long-term social and economic trends. A good example of rapid market change was seen during the time of the Gulf War, where tourism suffered a dramatic reduction in demand. The opportunities deriving from such a market alteration are minimal, while longer term market change, such as the growth in weekend breaks, and the increase in the number of pensioners with disposable income, provide the hospitality operator with potential new markets.

In analysing business opportunities, the operator will be looking at local and national trends, at local developments and developing markets. Operators concerned with new local markets may spend some time obtaining information and developing contacts to maximise sales opportunities.

Analysing business threats

Threats to a business can vary from short term to long term. On a wider scale, overall business may be affected by the prevailing economic climate, government legislation or a decline in a particular market. On a smaller scale, threats to business may occur by the emergence of increased local competition and the loss of skilled staff. The operator seeks to identify what will threaten business, both in the short and long term, forecasting how such threats will affect business performance.

Use of SWOT analysis

Such analysis can be snapshot activity, in that a picture of the business is taken at one time to establish an indication of how it should operate in the near future. However, while this method has some short-term advantages, the majority of operators continually assess existing and potential business, enabling them to deal positively with market changes.

Hospitality operators, therefore, utilise such analysis alongside other business considerations to identify the basis for plans to achieve business objectives.

HOW ARE THE BUSINESS OBJECTIVES TO BE ACHIEVED?

Having identified by careful analysis appropriate market opportunities, the operator then needs to decide how best to maximise on these opportunities. A marketing plan is designed, identifying the appropriate marketing tools, timing, responsibilities, costings and evaluation elements that will lead to the achievement of objectives with a cost-effective result.

SALES AND MARKETING ACTION PLANS
The sales and marketing plan will have sections dealing with the particular sector or sectors of the business the operator is targeting. It will normally include the identification of methods, costs, targets and responsibilities. While for larger companies such a detailed plan would be fairly extensive, for small units or for individual projects the plan would be relatively simple.

The industry does utilise external marketing consultants to both analyse business and develop action plans. Additionally, the Department of Trade and Industry (DTI) marketing initiative assists hospitality operators in the cost of such planning.

One example of the DTI marketing initiative is the Rutland Hotel, Sheffield. Robert Harwood, the General Manager, made use of consultants identified by the DTI to assist with the development and marketing of the hotel's restaurant.

'We had identified some years ago that there was a need for a certain style of restaurant within the area. About 60–70 per cent of our residents utilised the restaurant, and due to the location of the hotel and ease of access for guests to the restaurant, we believed we could capitalise on this opportunity.

'Following reports, advice and technical assistance from the consultant, we refurbished the restaurant and restyled the menu. One of our strengths was the friendly atmosphere, value for money and generous portions which was identified as "positive Yorkshire virtues".

'The consultant assisted us in analysing our strengths and focusing our marketing activities. A humorous menu was designed, which proved to be a valuable marketing tool in promoting our "Yorkshire Restaurant". Customer feedback, which is obtained by the utilisation of comment cards, has been extremely favourable, and the restaurant and other hotel facilities has gained considerable additional business.

'Overall, the consultant was able to focus our attention on the key aspects of the business which, while we were aware of them, needed a proper push to get us started.'

The Elton Hotel in South Yorkshire is a well-established operation with a mix of commercial and private business. Following considerable refurbishment of the premises, including the addition of extra accommodation, the owner, Peter Keary, was keen to develop the business further and adapt marketing and sales practices to a changing customer base.

'As a relatively small operation, we had neither the time nor perhaps the expertise to both investigate and initiate marketing opportunities. Use was made of the DTI marketing initiative. Following discussions with representatives from the DTI, we identified marketing consultants appropriate to our needs. It was vital that in addition to possessing the appropriate skills and expertise, the consultant was reasonably local and one with whom we could work.

'The DTI initiative provided us with approximately nine days of direct consultancy, and has assisted us in developing focused plans for the next two and a half years.'

Following initial discussion the consultant conducted an in-depth review of the business, looking at the strengths, weaknesses and opportunities to agreed terms of reference.

'The consultant was able to look objectively at my business and point out both strengths and faults, which due to being involved in the day-to-day operation, I was not fully aware of.'

The initial review was followed by more detailed analysis of current marketing and sales activity and local competition. Out of this analysis came a detailed marketing plan which covered:

- general sales and marketing activity;
- a proposal to join a marketing consortium;
- the redesign of sales literature;
- the collection and utilisation of guest data;
- the projection of forecasted business;
- promotional events;
- public relations.

All these elements were costed with proposed budgets set for certain of the areas.

'Such a proposal allowed for the correct planning and implementation of the recommendations.'

For a unit, such information and assistance can be vital in maintaining and developing appropriate business. It allows the operator to focus on key elements of activities, and by including cost and evaluation mechanisms provides the operator with assistance and guidelines for further marketing and sales activity.

'It is of vital importance to utilise specialists for such activities, even down to the design and content of sales literature. Inappropriate methods or materials can prove very negative in respect of returns.'

SALES AND MARKETING ACTION PLANS:
COMPONENT STAGES AND ELEMENTS

• *Identified sales opportunities* setting of measurable targets	Market segments identified Forecast of additional revenue
• *Selection of marketing tools*	Sales literature, advertising, direct mail, incentive schemes, promotional launches, PR and related costs
• *Timing and location*	Positioning and promotion target dates
• *Responsibilities*	Identified individuals teams, consultants, agencies plus staff training
• *Delivery*	Delivery into market place and at targets
• *Evaluation*	Costs against actual increased business Customer feedback Staff feedback

Fig. 2.1

EXAMPLE OF A BASIC SALES AND MARKETING ACTION PLAN

Outline. The 'Kincald Hotel' has identified potential for increased business from a local business park, especially in the area of lunchtime restaurant trade, with additional sales opportunities in the areas of accommodation and conference markets.

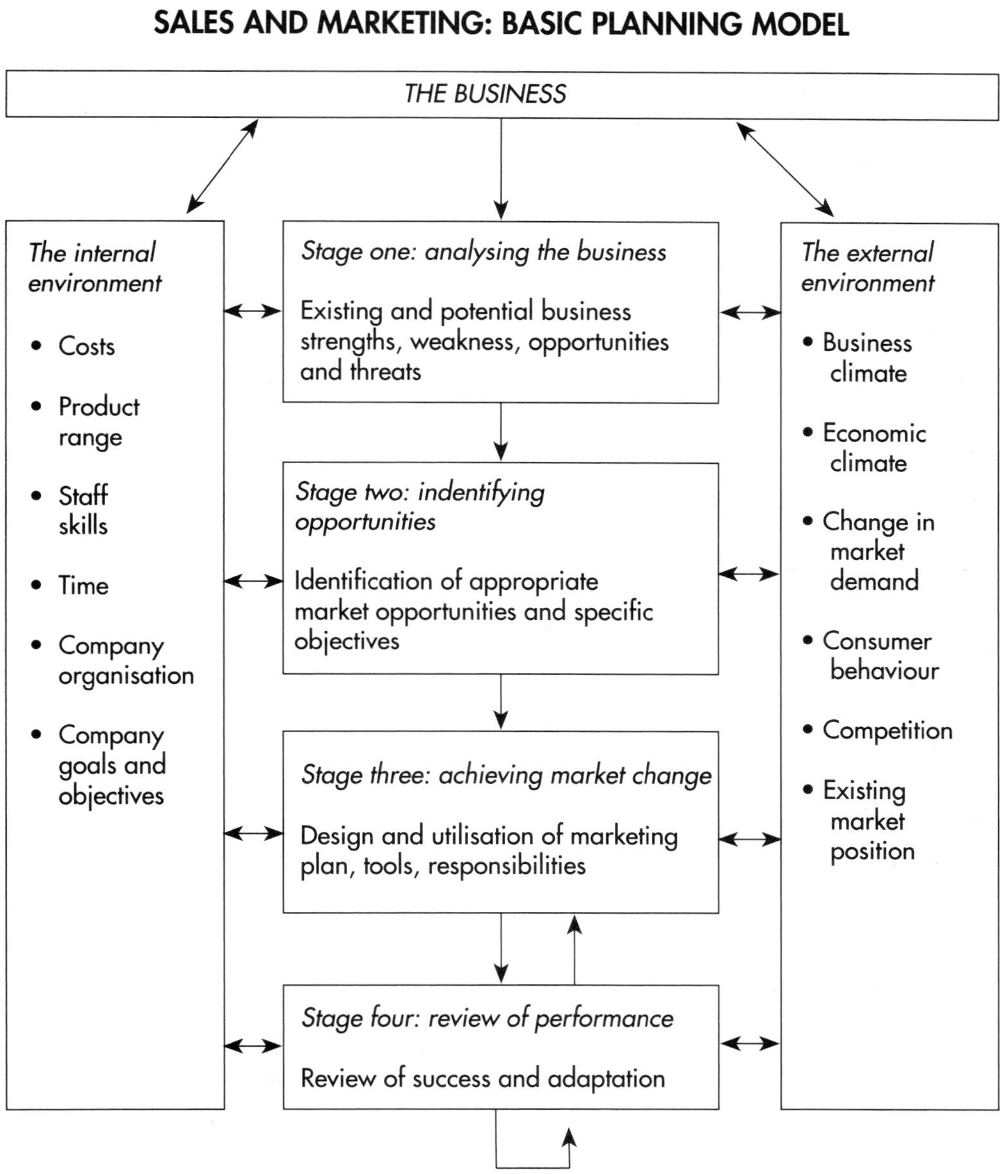

SALES AND MARKETING: BASIC PLANNING MODEL

THE BUSINESS

The internal environment

- Costs
- Product range
- Staff skills
- Time
- Company organisation
- Company goals and objectives

Stage one: analysing the business

Existing and potential business strengths, weakness, opportunities and threats

Stage two: indentifying opportunities

Identification of appropriate market opportunities and specific objectives

Stage three: achieving market change

Design and utilisation of marketing plan, tools, responsibilities

Stage four: review of performance

Review of success and adaptation

The external environment

- Business climate
- Economic climate
- Change in market demand
- Consumer behaviour
- Competition
- Existing market position

Fig. 2.2

Notes: The basic model in Figure 2.2 illustrates the stages and considerations involved in planning sales and marketing activity. Whatever the size of the company, the prime considerations should be the activity and the acievement of objectives.

Aims of plan:

- To raise awareness of hotel's accommodation and conference facilities.
- To increase restaurant lunchtime trade by 20 per cent.

Target: Local companies.

Methods:

- A promotional lunch to company secretaries by written invitation with telephone follow up.
- A direct mailshot to companies comprising a personally signed letter and restaurant menu.
- Follow-up calls to targeted companies by the hotel manager or restaurant manager to ascertain demand, and give an invitation to the clients to sample the restaurant and view conference facilities.
- The creation of an incentive scheme for conference booking, with reductions related to regular bookings.
- An advertisement in the local business newsletter on the restaurant.
- All new clients to be greated personally by the restaurant manager or hotel manager.

Costs:

- the promotion lunch;
- the promotion letter;
- the incentive discount scheme;
- the advertisement in the newsletter;
- the review scheme.

Evaluation:

- an alteration in restaurant sales (costs);
- an increase in conference bookings (costs);
- a six-month review on new established clients.

CONCLUSION

Effective planning should occur in all aspects of hospitality operations. The planning process applied to sales and marketing activity is a fairly simple one, yet its importance should not be underestimated. Whether a business is suffering a reduction in demand or enjoying growth, the role of planning is both to assist business performance and maintain profitable growth. Although at certain times, planning may be concentrated on survival strategies.

To achieve this, the operator is required to consider a wide range of factors that are affecting, or will affect, the business. An understanding of the position of the company in the market place, its present and forecasted business mix and the factors that affect a particular product range, service or facility cycle of profitability is required.

The following sections in this chapter will look at other considerations related to the initial planning of sales and marketing activities, including market positioning and segmentation, the product life cycle and the marketing mix.

MARKET POSITIONING AND SEGMENTATION

MARKET POSITIONING

The position a company or unit holds in the market place relates to both the range, style, price and promotion of its products and services, and the level of demand for its services. While its performance in the market place is related to a variety of economic factors, its position is related to consumer perceptions of its worth. To explain this in more detail, it is useful to examine the Fortes Group, which comprises various divisions, hotels, contract catering, restaurants and other operations. Its hotel division with some 338 hotels and over 29,000 bedrooms in the UK, ranks first among the top 50 UK hotel groups.

Its market position in the UK could be conceived as the strongest, at least in terms of potential occupancy. However, within the division are sub-groups comprising Fortes: Posthouses, Forte Crest, Forte Heritage, Forte Grand, Forte Exclusive and Travelodge. The restructing process Fortes went through in 1991–92 attempted, among other things, to create a rationalisation, both in company terms and in respect of the consumers' viewpoint. Fixing certain groups within the market place with the aim to attract particular market groups, Travelodge currently is in the restaurant division as an operator offering accommodation to the traveller. It is in its basic form no different from a Fortes Crest, Heritage or Exclusive Hotel. All offer rooms and facilities for the traveller seeking accommodation.

However, there are considerable differences between the groups. All attempt to attract certain types of market groups, and their pricing, promotion, facilities and services are aimed at establishing a lead position within certain market sectors against other competitors.

While all hotel operators compete for customers, the competition is for various segments of the overall market. The move towards the branding of hotel groups has been apparent since the early 1990s, with companies streamlining their operations with the identification of particular branded operations attempting to capitalise on effective promotion and particular market sector growths.

This rather complicated restructuring is evidence of the theory that the consumer relates more easily to particular brands. Operators attempt to position themselves in the market place to attract particular market sectors.

POSITIONING A COMPANY OR UNIT

Having completed initial research, operators seek to establish a position within the market place where they have the best possible chance of maximising market opportunities.

The range of the products, services and facilities, the physical location of their premises, the quality and style of the establishment, and the pricing and promotion of products and services are all designed to capture particular

Fig. 2.3

AN EXAMPLE OF QUALITY 'TARGETED PROMOTIONAL MATERIAL' PROMOTING FACILITIES AT HILTON HOTELS

market groups against other competitors.

Whether the operator is concerned with budget-style overnight accommodation, high-cost food and beverage provision, banqueting and conference trade, leisure breaks, commercial and business trade or five-star luxury tourist accommodation, the aim is to establish in the consumer's eyes an awareness of the company or unit and its range of products, services and facilities.

Therefore, market positioning basically works along the following lines:

- existing and potential markets are identified;
- facilities, services and goods are provided;
- awareness-raising activity;
- sales and marketing activities;
- adaptations to market change.

Larger companies will also seek to position themselves by the number of particular units, establishing what could be referred to as lead market position

due to accessibility of their provision. However, the number of units does not necessarily equate with success or profitability. This was certainly evident in the early 1990s, where the recession and other factors caused many hospitality operators to curtail their development plans.

ALTERATION TO POSITIONING

Smaller companies and independent operators face similar problems with positioning. When the economic climate changes, market changes will force many to readjust to new situations. Additionally, danger exists in creating the wrong image in the eye of the consumer. For instance, the recession of 1991/92 had various effects on the hospitality industry. Operators who before had traded on high-cost, high-quality factors, found themselves attempting to alter their market position, attempting to dispute the factor of high cost.

The opportunity to reposition a unit in the market place or to specific market segments is a problem with both practical and cost implications for the operator. It may simply involve targeted sales and marketing activity or a complete change in the style, facilities, goods and services offered.

Many of the fast-food operators have had to adapt to such change. In the 1960s and 1970s, Wimpey Bars were predominant in many high streets, in the 1980s Kentucky Fried Chicken, and in the mid-1980s to 1990s McDonalds.

All of these operators had to alter their style of operation and range of goods as the market changed. It will be interesting to see whether the growth in pizza houses, Pizza Hut, Pizzaland, and the emergence of branded restaurants along the lines of Harvester, will suffer the same fate. This aspect is dealt with in more detail in 'The concept of branding' (below).

CONCLUSION

It can be seen that one particular market which all hospitality operators seek to satisfy does not exist. Rather the market is made up of different groups and individuals who the operators need to identify and target effectively.

It is also important to realise that individual units will also need to target particular market segments for various elements of their provision. Quite simply, while the company or unit may be positioned positively within the market, elements of their provision may not be, and every area of provision requires marketing and selling.

The hospitality operator needs to be aware of all the different market groups, which are often referred to as market segments. The following section deals with this aspect.

MARKET SEGMENTATION

In 'Markets and customers' (above), the need for the effective identification of customer needs – the first stage in the marketing activity cycle – was identified.

In the previous section, the concept of market position was outlined, identifying how hospitality operators seek to position themselves to attract particular market groups, or segments of these groups. It is now important to look in more detail at the concept of market segmentation and explain the importance of understanding the role of market segmentation in respect of sales and marketing activity.

THE CONCEPT OF SEGMENTATION

Studies of the overall consumer market quickly identify that no one similar or homogeneous group exists, that is, one overall group with the same backgrounds, needs, expectations and buying behaviour patterns. Rather the total market, that is, individuals and groups who may purchase goods, facilities or services, can be separated into sub-groups or segments. The sub-groups or segments will have varying needs and requirements, and while they will be made up of individuals, certain patterns of needs or buying behaviour can be identified.

The separation of groups into more easily targeted segments has developed through various stages over the years. Hospitality operators utilise the knowledge of those segments in a variety of ways, both in creating facilities and marketing those facilities.

The theory is that with more detailed knowledge and understanding of the needs of particular segments, the operator can develop appropriate marketing strategies to attract and satisfy individuals and groups from various or specific market segments.

Therefore, it is important to differentiate between the two aspects mentioned. Segmentation theory refers to the theoretical groupings of individuals with certain common needs or buying behaviour. Segmentation strategy refers to the sales and marketing activities operators undertake in an attempt to reach certain groups or segments.

DEFINITION OF SEGMENTATION

The separation of the overall market into reasonably homogeneous groups for the purpose of identifying and satisfying their particular needs.

THE RELEVANCE OF MARKETING SEGMENTATION TO THE HOSPITALITY INDUSTRY

There exists considerable debate about the importance of segmentation. While it can be seen that by identifying more clearly the particular needs and requirements of particular groups, the operator will be more able to provide the appropriate marketing mix to attract and satisfy particular customer needs, there do exist weaknesses in arguing that operators can rely solely on this strategy.

At best, segmentation provides approximate indicators of potential buying behaviour. The groups, however they are established, are made up of individuals whose buying behaviour is affected by a variety of socio-economic and psychological factors.

Market research on the buying patterns of particular groups is conducted across a wide range of goods, services and facilities. Historial purchase patterns are co-related to potential purchase patterns. Such research, however, only provides an approximate indication of potential consumer behaviour.

Accepting these weaknesses, the industry utilises knowledge of potential consumer buying behaviour in a variety of ways:

- To identify the need for a particular facility and its best location.
- To identify potential changes in market demand for certain products or facilities.
- To identify the appropriate marketing mix that will attract and satisfy particular customers.
- To identify trends in buying behaviour for a particular group or groups.
- To identify groups who would not wish to purchase particular goods or services.
- To identify where the level of demand is insufficient, thereby making it non-cost effective for concentrated targeting.
- To identify groups whose type of demand is inappropriate to the operator.

Examples of these could be:

- Locating an up-market restaurant in an area where sufficient numbers of individuals with disposable income reside.
- A hotel group that develops longer-term strategies to adapt its facilities to changing demand.
- A restaurant chain that fixes its products, placing, promotion and pricing relevant to the customer groups it seeks to satisfy.
- A conference facility that, as a result of the identification of particular group needs, decides to upgrade specific facilities.
- A luxury hotel that aims and targets its sales and marketing activity at particular groups, thereby not wasting costly activity on market groups that have little need of its facilities.
- A hotel whose other main clientele (market) would not 'accept' other groups within the facility.

The industry will also utilise segmentation theory and strategy in order to:

- prepare marketing plans and activities;
- identify the most appropriate type of advertising or promotion;
- set levels of staff and related skills;
- plan and forecast budgets.

The relevance of market segmentation theory and strategy is recognisable for the industry. Whatever type of operation exists, there is a need to maximise sales and marketing activity, and this can be satisfied partly by the utilisation of targeted marketing. Hospitality operators' strategies in approaching market segments fall into three basic types:

Undifferentiated or mass marketing. Where sales and marketing activity is aimed at the overall market and little differentiation is defined between the various segments. This method is not utilised a great deal by the industry.

Differentiated or selective marketing. When the operator seeks to attract a variety of groups and markets utilising a variety of methods.

Concentrated or niche marketing. Where the operator seeks to target a fairly specific market segment, usually with a particular product, facility or service.

If you look through national media, you will see examples of all of the above. Attempt to identify what group or market segment the operator is seeking to attract, and the differences in the messages for different groups.

MARKET SEGMENT GROUPS

There exist a variety of ways in which groups or market segments are identified. It could be by age, gender, location, socio-economic status, attitudes, lifestyle, benefits and product utilisation. Such groupings attempt to identify common needs, expectations and buying behaviour. A hospitality operator may identify that his customer mix for accommodation across a year is broken down into:

50 per cent business or commercial trade;
30 per cent tourists;
20 per cent travel trade.

However, this generalisation of segments does not give precise information about them. For instance, the 50 per cent business trade may be concentrated into certain trading periods and times. The individuals within this overall business segment may also be separated by age, gender and product utilisation.
More detailed analysis will identify other particular aspects, which will further complicate the analysis. For example, of the 50 per cent business trade:

30 per cent are identified as returning customers;
45 per cent are booked by their particular companies;
40 per cent pay by company account;
25 per cent stay two nights or more;
38 per cent utilise the hotel restaurant;
48 per cent come from over 150 miles distance;
28 per cent are male;
32 per cent were attending company-organised conferences and 20 per cent of the conference bookings came via a conference booking agency.

Such analysis, which is easily available through the use of computers, provides the operator with historical data on users, and may also indicate trends for future segment needs (product usage segmentation). As explained, various factors are utilised to identify particular market segments (consumer segmentation):

- the source of the booking, for example, company, agency;
- socio-economic grouping;
- the characteristics of the group, for example, age, gender, geographical location;
- product utilisation, for example, weekend breaks, conferences, functions, individual accommodation;
- duration of utilisation, for example, the number or frequency of bookings.

Operators will decide how best to group market segments for their particular businesses.

Whatever the criteria utilised for identifying groups, the underlying considerations for the hospitality operator are that groups must be:

- of appropriate size;
- accessible;
- contain appropriate demand; and be
- profitable.

Busy operators do not sit down and plan to reach so many people aged between eighteen and twenty-five, or all householders in a particular location. This is usually the reserve of specialist marketing and advertising agencies. Rather they utilise the knowledge of market segments to target sales and marketing activities more effectively.

Conclusion
The concept, theory and strategy of segmentation is a fairly complex one. While improvements are being made in the science of segmentation all the time, there do exist weaknesses. Hospitality operators increasingly make use of specialist agencies and technology to enhance their sales and marketing planning and activities. Such utilisation is another effective element in the sales and marketing activity cycle.

Other considerations, such as the emergence of branded marketing and the concept of the product life cycle, must also be analysed.

THE PRODUCT LIFE CYCLE

You have seen that the hospitality market is not one neat, homogeneous group, rather it is made up of a variety of sub-groups or segments. The needs of these groups change for a variety of reasons, and the industry attempts to identify these changes and satisfy them by altering or adapting its product range – the mix of services, facilities and goods.

While the need for accommodation, food and drink remain, the type of demand may alter not only over a fairly short time span, but also over longer periods. Therefore, products have what is referred to as a 'life span'. This life span often exhibits certain characteristics in respect of market demand and profitability. Products are said to go through a cycle of characteristics – referred to as the 'product life cycle'.

While this theory has certain weaknesses, a basic knowledge of it can assist the hospitality operator in longer term planning and identifying more cost-effective marketing and sales activity.

A DEFINITION OF THE PRODUCT LIFE CYCLE
The stages products go through in relation to cost, profitability and demand.

Products are generally said to go through four basic stages in their life span:

- *introduction or launch:* the product is introduced to the market;
- *growth:* sales grow with increased customer awareness;
- *maturity:* sales plateau;
- *decline:* sales reduce as other products are introduced and customer behaviour alters.

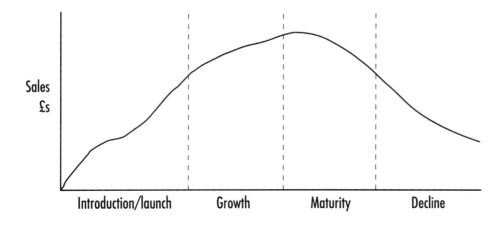

Fig. 2.4
GRAPH SHOWING THE FOUR BASIC STAGES IN THE PRODUCT LIFE CYCLE

INTRODUCTION OR LAUNCH

Here a new or adapted product is brought to the market – usually following on from the research and analysis of consumer needs. Associated with such launches are increased costs, such as spending on advertising and promotion, in order to create appropriate customer awareness of the product. The operator may be introducing a completely new product, attempting to create a 'niche' or leading position within the market place. Or the operator may be following other companies who have introduced successful products.

GRANADA STUDIOS TOUR LIMITED

Quay Street, Manchester M60 9EA.
Telephone 061-832 9090. Facsimile 061-953 0296

Dear Event Organiser

I am delighted to enclose for your interest and information a copy of the new promotional leaflet for the Victoria & Albert Hotel.

This exciting 132 bedroom property opens in central Manchester in October 1992, and is already creating considerable interest.

Following the success of Granada Studios Tour it was felt that a quality hotel serving the needs of both the business and leisure community would be very popular and initial response to this essentially "different" hotel has been swift and encouraging.

Should you require a more detailed personal presentation, or indeed simply clarification of rates and availability then please do not hesitate to contact me, I would be delighted to help.

I hope I can welcome you to the Victoria & Albert Hotel in the near future.

Yours sincerely

Alan MacGregor
SALES & MARKETING DIRECTOR

Ref: V.A.2.

Registered office Atherton Street Manchester M60 9E

GST/010/01

A MEMBER OF GRAN

I would like the following information about Victoria and Albert Hotel	
Accommodation: Individual	☐
Group	☐
Speciality Packages	☐
Restaurant Menus	☐
Conference/Banqueting Details	☐
Other requirements	☐

COMPANY

NAME

POSITION

ADDRESS

POSTCODE

TEL NO:

APPEALING TO THE *EYE* AND TO THE *PALATE*.

THE GRANDFATHER CLOCK strikes the hour as the barman removes the froth from a pewter tankard with a wooden spatula in **Watson's Bar**.

The heavy drapes, the glint of gilt from the leather volumes in Sherlock's bookcases and you're taken back to a time where the pace of life was only as fast as a brewery dray or Hansom cab.

Now is the time for you to savour our extensive range of malt whiskies or alternatively enjoy a pint of cask-conditioned ale.

THE SHERLOCK HOLMES RESTAURANT

Under the eagle eye of the *Maitre d'* nothing passes unnoticed in the stylish period atmosphere of our elegant restaurant.

Soft classical music blends with the clink of fine cut crystal glasses as waiters in full tails serve the finest haute cuisine.

Whether you choose an authentic traditional Victorian dish from our *à la Carte* menu or the chef's speciality *table d'hôte* you can rest assured our experienced sommelier will ensure your choice of meal is perfectly complemented by a fine wine from the superbly stocked cellar.

Styled on Granada's successful detective series starring Michael Gambon, Café Maigret has all the atmosphere of a busy Parisian Brasserie. The smell of freshly ground coffee and hot croissants fill the air, while down in the cellar a unique selection of French regional wines are waiting to be savoured.

Café Maigret serves light snacks throughout the day, popular for a continental breakfast and a sociable meeting place in the evening for residents, local professionals and celebrities alike.

5

6

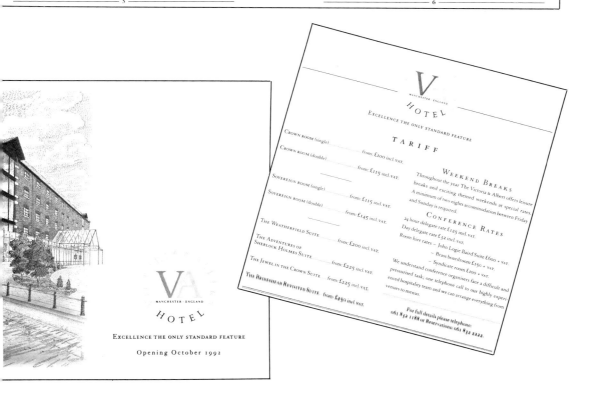

Fig. 2.5

PRE-OPENING PUBLICITY MATERIAL FOR THE VICTORIA AND ALBERT HOTEL IN MANCHESTER

One example of this was the introduction of budget-style accommodation in the mid- to late 1980s – the travel lodge type operation. Market research had indicated an increased demand for accommodation with specific forecasted growth in quality, low-cost accommodation situated in convenient locations for the traveller. Observers of this market will have noticed the expansion in provision with companies such as Granada Lodge, Welcome Break and Quality Inns all entering the market.

FACTORS TO BE CONSIDERED
The risks associated with introducing totally new products are great, but they are minimised with appropriate and effective planning. However, while major operators complete detailed planning, it is not until the market is tested and actual demand is realised that risks are reduced.

GROWTH

At this stage, demand for the product increases as it 'takes off'. Sales increase and, if the planning has been correct, so do profits. Customer awareness increases and the competition (other operators) starts to enter the market with a similar product.

FACTORS TO BE CONSIDERED
As demand increases, the operator is able to open additional outlets. The market becomes price sensitive, with several operators competing for the same market. Again, the budget-style accommodation boom of the late 1980s and early 1990s saw competitors attempting to differentiate their products, through prices, style and facilities. Formula One entered the UK market in the early 1990s with a very low-price strategy. It is too early to determine that the demand for the product has justified the strategy.

As competition increases, the original innovator or leader is forced to look closely at the product and decide how best to deal with the problems effective competition brings.

MATURITY

As effective competition increases, the market becomes saturated, that is, demand starts to level off with consumers, who, having tested the products on offer, tend to stay with their brand preference – the supplier they like the most.

FACTORS TO BE CONSIDERED
As the market share begins to level out, an increase in sales can only occur through alterations to buyer behaviour or the product itself. Operators will attempt to differentiate their particular brands in a variety of ways.

Communication with consumers will increase and minor adaptions will be made to the basic product.

DECLINE

As demand declines through increased competition or change in consumer behaviour, the operator faces several problems. Sales and, therefore, profitability fall, the cost of promotion increases and the opening of new units offering the same product becomes riskier.

FACTORS TO BE CONSIDERED

Both the original operator and market followers will consider strategies, including withdrawals from the market, adaptation of the product, aggressive marketing and possible mergers and competitor buy-outs. One could consider the then Trust House Fortes buy-out of Happy Eater to coincide with the Little Chef chain, as an example of this latter strategy.

CONCLUSION

The classic cycle identified above, while useful in identifying a general picture is generally considered too simplistic in today's market. Consideration should be given to the following:

- All products differ and will go through these stages in varying time scales.
- Hospitality operators often have a variety of products which may be at different points in the cycle.
- The cycle will be positively or adversely affected by a range of external factors.
- A declining product may be relaunched successfully with only minor adaptations.
- Increased sales and marketing activity for a declining product may identify new users.

In the 1950s and 1960s, holiday camp operators like Butlins, Warner and Pontins all experienced rapid growth. The decline in demand for such products came about by a variety of socio-economic factors. The overall market declined rapidly in the 1970s and early 1980s; however, with adaptation to the product, its packaging, pricing and promotion, demand has now returned. Whether the growth in more sophisticated facilities, such as Center Parcs, will affect this growth remains to be seen.

THE RELEVANCE OF PRODUCT LIFE CYCLE TO SALES AND MARKETING ACTIVITY

While it can be seen that the classic product life cycle has many weaknesses, its relevance to the industry remains, if only as an indicator of the need for appropriate planning. The hospitality operator utilises many other planning devices to maintain sales and profitability.

The products an operator offers are designed to attract a variety of customers. This is activated by continually identifying market segment needs and creating the most appropriate mix of products to satisfy these needs.

The following section will look in more detail at the concept of branding in relation to marketing and sales activity.

THE CONCEPT OF BRANDING

The concept of branding is not a new one to the hospitality industry. Companies and units have for some time attempted to create a certain image for their products in the eyes of potential consumers. As a marketing technique, it is used widely by companies across the business spectrum. One can readily recognise such high-yield consumer products as washing powder, toothpaste, chocolate bars, soft drinks and cars, as branded goods. Branded goods are products whose name conjures up in consumers' eyes certain positive perceptions of worth, benefit, value, quality and effectiveness. Conversely consumers may perceive certain products to have low worth or value.

Consider the following: Rolls-Royce car, Volvo car, Marks & Spencer's food range, the *Sun* newspaper. What image does each brand conjure up in your eyes. For a Rolls-Royce car it may be status and cost. For a Volvo car it may be safety. For Marks & Spencer's food range it may be higher cost but quality. For the *Sun* newspaper it may be easy reading!

While a Rolls-Royce is, after all, just a car, and the Marks & Spencer's food range just food, each product or brand possess the inherent ability to affect how consumers perceive its worth. Its position in the market place, its pricing and promotion and packaging will all have an effect on the consumer. For the hospitality industry, this concept is just as appropriate. Consider the following products. What image is created in your mind?

- Kentucky Fried Chicken;
- The Savoy Hotel;
- Little Chef;
- Berni Inns;
- Butlins.

The image the brand name conjures up for you may differ from the image your friends have of the brand name. If their perceptions of a particular product differ from yours, consider what has affected their response. Is it the effect of advertising, personal experience of the product or, perhaps, perceptions gained from others?

DEFINITION OF BRANDING
Branding is the provision of a name or image to a product assisting its positioning within the market place.

THE RELEVANCE OF BRANDING TO THE HOSPITALITY INDUSTRY

Hospitality operators attempt to differentiate their products from those of competitors. They make use of branding to identify in potential consumers' eyes a positive image of their products. This is particularly true of the larger operators. They attempt to create brand loyalty by opening units with common product ranges, fixed prices and service styles. Having tested the product, customers will know the standards the operator provides, whichever unit they visit.

American operators, such as Holiday Inns, expanded world wide in the 1960s–80s using this strategy. Wherever you went in the world, staying in a Holiday Inn would hold no surprises. Restaurant chains, such as Pizzahut, Berni, Beefeater and Harvester, all utilise this strategy to some degree of success.

Branding creates an identity not only for individual products but also for companies with multiple units.

'The philosophy behind the concept is offering the guest a high standard of food and service to a predetermined specification. The guest can then quickly identify, or identify with, the restaurant chain and so is confident that he or she will receive the same product whether visiting a house in Scotland or Cornwall.'
Source: Janet Maltby, Toby Restaurants.

THE ADVANTAGES OF BRANDING

Accepting the fact that branding clearly identifies a product or product range and ideally differentiates it positively from other competitors, what other advantages does it possess for hospitality operators?

SET UP

- The operator faces reduced risk by creating additional units from a tried-and-tested formula.
- Set-up costs are reduced as design and layout considerations are standard.
- Provisioning, staffing and equipping costs are reduced, too.

OPERATION

- Costs are reduced due to common operating procedures.

PROMOTION AND ADVERTISING

- Due to the common format, centralised promotion sales and advertising material can be produced, reducing costs and, possibly, increasing impact.
- As customer perceptions already exist, the operator has a captive market in that consumers are aware of the product and, hopefully, have a positive image of its worth or value.

Branding then can positively assist operators – particularly the larger companies in a variety of ways. However, while the concept of branding is widely accepted and utilised, its use does not guarantee success in the market place. There exists a variety of problems concerned with this commonality of approach which must be considered.

THE DISADVANTAGES OF BRANDING

CONSUMERS' PERCEPTION

- Whatever styles of promotion and packaging have been utilised, there is always the risk that sufficient numbers of consumers will have a negative image of the product. This was the case with some holiday-camp operators in the 1970s.
- As the market demand alters, the range of products may become dated: unsophisticated, 'old fashioned' or seen as always the same. The novelty has, perhaps, worn off and consumers will move elsewhere to seek other products. Fast-food operators specialising in a fairly small product range face this particular problem.
- The consumer may perceive the product as high quality, but also of too high a cost. In periods of recession, this may result in considerably reduced demand.
- Competitors who enter the same market may offer an improved product or product range, forcing the original operator to quickly adapt its range or undertake aggressive and costly promotion. Bernis, who originated the 'Steak Bar' concept, faced this problem when other competitors, such as Beefeaters, Cavaliers and Harvester, entered the market.

SIZE

Individual operators or companies with small numbers of units cannot readily utilise this method. Their particular product brand identity is, perhaps, more difficult to create.

Costs

Operators designing and developing a brand have extremely high set-up costs with the inherent risk that the concept may not be accepted by the market.

Conclusion

You can see that branding has particular relevance for the hospitality operator. Sales and marketing activity can be concentrated on developing and maintaining a positive identity and image for the consumer. Large operators can utilise longer-term cost savings to increase market penetration and establish clearly defined market segments for targeted sales and promotion. Branding can also assist the customer by identifying a clearly defined product, which increases confidence. It assists operators in positioning themselves in the market to take up developing market opportunities.

However, branding is not without its weaknesses, including its dependence on brand loyalty. Fortes' decision to restructure its hotel division (see 'Market positioning and segmentation', above) is an example of rebranding on a large scale. The costs and risks were high, and many of its units which underwent rebranding have had to work to recreate brand loyalty as their customer base has altered.

This is where the effectiveness of the product range will be of increased importance. The next section describes the importance of evaluating marketing and sales activity.

Evaluating success in marketing and sales

Effective marketing and sales planning and activity includes elements of measurability and evaluation. At the outset of planning, hospitality operators seek to identify sales opportunities that will, if targeted correctly, become profitable.

After a period of marketing and sales activity, hospitality operators will seek to analyse business and identify in precise terms the amount of profit or return. While there are circumstances when marketing activity is not profit centred, for instance, in general, untargeted awareness raising campaigns, the basic rule is that marketing activity should give a profitable return.

Accepting that all marketing and sales activities have been planned effectively (see 'The planning process', above), the operator should have built in appropriate mechanisms for evaluating success. This section concerns the reasons and methods of evaluating success that hospitality operators utilise.

THE COST FACTOR

Successful marketing and sales is usually the outcome of detailed planning. Such planning requires staff time and facilities. Additional costs exist, including possible fees to professional agencies, advertising costs, printing and mailing costs, the cost of discounting and the risk cost that the activity will result in negative sales. Therefore, as considerable costs and risks are undertaken, the operator will want to see that these costs have at worst been met, and at best resulted in genuine increased profits.

Let us take an example of a hotel seeking to increase accommodation utilisation over a certain period by offering a discount scheme. Breaking this down in terms of analysis:

Marketing and sales costs	£2,500.00
Identified increased revenue	£6,400.00
Gross profit	£3,900.00

The campaign has been successful, generating a reasonable gross profit and presumably additional new customers who, hopefully, will return. However, let us take this cost/revenue analysis a little further.

Gross profit	£3,900.00
Less fixed costs	£1,400.00
Net profit	£2,500.00

Still, the return is reasonable, the operator has identified new customers, and for a small outlay has added to potential further repeat business. Now let us add more detail about both costs and revenue.

Net profit	£2,500.00
Less cost of discounting	£1,200.00
'Genuine' return	£1,300.00

Now the return is seriously reduced and the success of the promotion is questionable. There is the added dimension that the customers may be quite willing to buy at the old price, and there may be existing customers who would resist a return to the old price.

This was certainly a factor after the Gulf War when prices were reduced drastically by some operators. One well quoted comment was: 'It's been easy to reduce prices, but it will be damned hard to put them back up again.'

CONCLUSION

Evaluating the costs against forecasted and actual revenue is of vital importance. However, unless costing is completed carefully with all aspects taken into account, then even what appears to be a success in a marketing and sales campaign may hide problems. Additionally, for many marketing and sales activities, the actual real return is difficult to identify. While profit is the most important factor, the operator utilises other types of analysis to evaluate success. The degree of sophistication of this analysis will obviously depend on both the type of promotion or campaign, and the type of operation.

CUSTOMER YIELD

A customer visiting a unit may have one main need, for example, overnight accommodation. However, the customer may additionally purchase a drink at the bar, eat in the restaurant, and make use of business facilities. This utilisation brings with it additional income. Let us use the example of the hotel providing discounted accommodation. Remember the last cost analysis showed only a marginal return.

Net profit	£2,500.00
Less cost of discounting	£1,200.00
Return on accommodation	£1,300.00
Add identified increased additional sales for period	500.00
Net yield or return	£1,800.00

The hotel operator is now happier. Overall sales have increased and net costs have decreased slightly due to increased accommodation utilisation.

CONCLUSION

It can be seen that more detailed analysis provides the operator with a clearer picture of whether the promotion was a success. However, such analysis requires the facilities to generate detailed information, which for some smaller companies may be difficult to obtain.

BUSINESS ANALYSIS

As indicated in the conclusion to customer yield analysis, the more detailed the analysis, the clearer the measurement of potential success or failure. Detailed analysis of the actual *business generated in respect of customer mix and new customers*, in addition to actual costs and revenue data, will provide the operator with a snapshot evaluation of performance.

Business analysis of accommodation promotion: of booked accommodation 25 per cent were new customers; 20 per cent were major business customers; and 5 per cent local business customers.

All of this may appear slightly confusing, and it is true that many operators would find such detailed analysis inappropriate and time consuming. The utilisation of computer technology in reservations and billing can assist.

CONCLUSION

The measurement of return of success from marketing and sales activity can be fairly basic or quite detailed. Costs against revenue must be the starting point, and one which most hospitality operators utilise within the planning process. More detailed analysis may also identify real return and, additionally, when a mix of advertising and promotion methods are made use of, the origin of the new business.

By identifying how the customers heard of the promotion, facility or unit, and what persuaded them to purchase, the operator will also obtain a clearer picture of which method is most effective. Within the assignment identified in Appendix A, you are asked to identify a marketing and sales activity and prepare an analysis on return.

CHAPTER REVIEW

This chapter has indicated the importance of effective planning, with sections related to the various strategies operators utilise in either bringing about a product or facility to the market, maintaining a position, increasing market share and positioning themselves within a market.

It is important to understand that while planning and strategy implementation are important, they do not guarantee profitable business for a company or unit. Operators will additionally make use of other marketing and sales activities in an attempt to achieve success.

Changes in the market place often catch companies ill prepared, and forecasts of business and identification of new sales opportunities are at best only indicators of potential growth and profit. It is the continuing analysis of actual sales, their origins, profit contribution and business mix that provide the operator with the real cycle of business – allowing more effective planning to take place.

In the 'boom' years of the late 1980s, a number of operators were successful despite not using planning techniques. However, today's highly competitive market makes effective planning and analysis very important, especially the aspect of identifying customer needs (covered in Chapter 3).

KEY POINTS

- Careful planning with identified aims and objectives is a key component of all aspects of hospitality management.

- Planning successful marketing campaigns relies on knowledge and understanding of all the factors that may affect the business.
- While the scope of planning activity will relate directly to the company or business, there exist three basic questions that can be asked:
  Where is the business now?
  Where will the business need to be in the future?
  How is this to be achieved?
- Every business will have its own strengths and weaknesses and will experience both threats to, and opportunities for, its development.
- Operators need to be aware of the position they hold within the market and need to understand how the characteristics of particular market segments can be satisfied.
- Market groups or segments will identify certain common characteristics; however, such groups are made up of individuals, a consideration which is becoming increasingly recognised.
- While market segments possess characteristics, so do the products the hospitality industry offers. An understanding of the stages in the life cycle of a product can assist decision making in relation to marketing and sales activities.
- There exists a trend towards the branding of products, attempting to create packages of products that will attract certain market groups.
- Planning is a continuous activity, and operators will seek to constantly review and evaluate forecasted performance against actual performance. By the effective evaluation of marketing and sales activities, the operator is able to identify further information as an aid to decision making.

QUESTIONS

- Explain the role of planning in relation to marketing and sales activities.
- Identify the factors that an operator should consider when undertaking planning.
- Explain the contribution a SWOT analysis can make to a business in respect of decision making.
- Explain the general market position of a company such as Travelodge, and why an understanding of its position is important in relation to long-term planning.
- What relevance does the concept of marketing segmentation have to the hospitality industry?
- List the stages of a product's life cycle identifying the key characteristics of each stage.
- What advantages exist in branding sectors of a company's operation?
- In what ways can an operator evaluate the 'success' of a marketing and sales activity?

CHAPTER THREE

IDENTIFYING CUSTOMER NEEDS

INTRODUCTION

Throughout Chapters 1 and 2, the importance of identifying customer needs has been described. This chapter deals with the topic in more detail.

On reading this chapter and completing the related questions and the particular assignment within Appendix A, the reader will be able to:

- Explain the importance of identifying market and customer needs and demands.
- Identify appropriate methods for the collection of this information.
- Understand the importance of the effective analysis of marketing research.
- Appreciate the role of forecasting in relation to product demand and provision.

For many individuals concerned with marketing and sales, the aspects outlined in this chapter are vitally important. For without clearly identifying customer needs, requirements and the nature and level of demand, how will operators know how to plan their businesses?

THE IMPORTANCE OF IDENTIFYING DEMAND

Chapter 3 identified the importance for hospitality operators of undertaking constant detailed analysis and review of potential and existing business. It is a factor which many within the industry identify as vital to maintaining and developing appropriate business. Hospitality operators require a constant stream of appropriate information related to the total business environment.

> DEFINITION OF IDENTIFYING DEMAND
> The systematic gathering, recording, analysis and utilisation of information related to all the factors which affect a business operator.

The key words within the definition are:

- *Systematic:* accepting that such activities should be carried out with clear aims in mind and with appropriate planning.
- *Analysis:* this indicates the importance of analysing the information gathered both to satisfy specific aims, and to provide data that can be utilised in decision making.
- *Utilisation:* this indicates that the information gathered must be appropriate to the organisation and can be made use of within further planning.

Sales and marketing decisions taken without reference to adequate and appropriate market research are more likely to fail than decisions based on systematic and detailed analysis. However, it would also be extravagant to claim that market research will guarantee success. Realistically it provides the operator with indicators of trends and opportunities – it is another weapon in the marketing and sales armoury.

Accepting its positive contribution to decision making, it is important to look in more detail at how the industry utilises such activities.

THE USE OF MARKET RESEARCH

The methods for identifying demand will be dealt with in more detail in the next section. However, it is important to recognise why the industry undertakes such activity.

We have seen that identifying customer needs is the first stage in the marketing process. Operators want to identify and forecast what customers may purchase and then satisfy these needs profitably. Increasingly, we see that operators utilise this customer or demand lead strategy. In times of high total demand, operators may be more likely to risk new ventures or products. Considerable capital investment in new ventures was seen in the late 1980s, for instance, in the luxury country house hotel market. The downturn in demand in the early 1990s led many operators into serious financial problems. The downturn in overall demand has strengthened the argument for more accurate identification of demand.

In addition to identification of general demand, the operator may utilise research for a variety of other reasons including:

- *Targeted research* to identify the potential of a particular product, its location, pricing and promotion.
- *Problem solving* to identify why a particular product or facility is suffering either slow or reduced demand.
- *Success identification* to identify the positive aspect of a product or facility, in an attempt to utilise the findings in other ventures.
- *Product launching* to identify whether a planned product or facility will attract the levels of business initially forecasted.

- *Potential users* to identify the geographical location of potential users of a planned or existing product so that more effective targeted marketing and promotion can occur.
- *Creation of business leads* to identify appropriate business leads for particular products and facilities so that more effective targeted selling can be planned.
- *Business analysis* to identify the type, range and source of existing business, assisting the identification of where marketing and sales activities should be concentrated on.
- *Customer satisfaction* to identify the degree of satisfaction or dissatisfaction of existing customers in relation to products, facilities and services provided.

Successful companies are often identified as ones which are close to, and understand, their customers; the ongoing detailed analysis of existing and potential business assists the development of this understanding.

It is important to realise that, for many of the larger operators who are separated more from their customers, the need for such analysis is increased. Additionally, while such research can be extremely costly, many smaller operators remain highly successful at identifying customer needs, utilising less expensive, but just as effective, market research techniques.

SUMMARY

The industry utilises market research in a systematic way to identify customer needs. The scale of such activity, while increasing, is dependent on the size of the company and its goals and aims. Its importance is its contribution to both short- and long-term planning and decision making. The next section will look in more detail at the methods the industry uses.

METHODS OF IDENTIFYING DEMAND

This section concentrates on the basic methods that are used to identify demand, the need for appropriate planning, and examples of how the industry utilises such processes.

THE PLANNING OF MARKET RESEARCH

Whatever the scale, the aim of market research should be to obtain appropriate information in the most cost effective way. Effective planning is, therefore, a primary consideration. Whether the operator is utilising external agencies, its own marketing and sales department or, in the case of smaller operators, individual skills, effective planning will help to make such activity a success. The

planning should cover all aspects of the research, including the identification of the problem, the setting of precise aims and objectives, the methodology utilised, the timing, the responsibilities, the cost, evaluation and analysis and potential utilisation.

This may at first appear a fairly complex approach and only appropriate for large-scale research. However, successful independent operators can, and do, utilise this approach to great effect on small-scale activity.

The purpose of planning is not to create complicated barriers to identify demand, but to assist the operator in achieving set goals, targets and to aid effective decision making. Figure 3.1 overleaf outlines the basic stages in this planning process.

Some operators may state: 'my planning is completed on the back of a matchbox'; while there may exist examples of ideas initiated in this manner, effective market research is the outcome of appropriate planning.

MARKET RESEARCH METHODS

It is important to make clear the difference between *marketing* research and *market* research. Marketing research is concerned with obtaining and analysing all aspects of the marketing process, while market research is concerned with identifying the characteristics of a particular market.

Both areas are complex and the detailed explanation of the science of market research is outside the scope of this text. Readers who wish to investigate this in more depth should refer to the reference section at the end of the book. Within the industry, the design and delivery of certain elements of research are often assigned to specialist companies and agencies. The majority of operators will not need to be aware of the intricacies of the methods involved.

THE PLANNING PROCESS FOR EFFECTIVE MARKETING RESEARCH

1 The identification of the problem	———— that is, reduced demand, product launc identification of potential demand
2 The identification of the aims for the research	———— that is, to identify potential business, to obtain existing customer feedback
3 The planning of activities	———— that is, action plan, timing
4 The identification of methodology	———— that is, market research questionnaires direct mail, data analysis, purchased marketing information
5 Setting responsibilities	———— that is, external agencies, operator's personnel
6 Budgeting	———— that is, setting constraints
7 Planning analysis and evaluation	———— that is, ensuring that appropriate analy will be undertaken
8 Identifying potential utilisation	———— that is, considering how the information will be utilised

Fig. 3.1

Market research methods can be separated into two types of approaches. First, methods utilised to reduce uncertainty when plans are being made and, secondly, to monitor performance when plans are in operation. The motives behind research can be categorised as follows:

- *Descriptive research:* research aimed at identifying particular problems.
- *Exploratory research:* research that attempts to identify hypotheses concerning market characteristics, that is, data on market size and consumer profiles.
- *Casual or diagnostic research:* research undertaken to test hypotheses generated by exploratory research.

Additionally, larger organisations may undertake ongoing research as evidence of their professional approach to business planning, while small businesses may undertake small-scale research to ascertain customer perceptions on the value or quality of service.

BASIC METHODS

The operator could utilise some or all of the following:

- telephone surveys;
- individual or personal interviews;
- mailed questionnaires;
- analysis of internal records or data;
- analysis of external research or data;
- competitor analysis;
- guest comment data.

For each of the above there exist certain 'rules' and considerations if the research is to be meaningful. Accepting that some of these methods may be best undertaken by specialist agencies, a brief outline of the possible use for each is detailed below. Readers should note that methods are not listed in order of either importance or effectiveness.

TELEPHONE SURVEY
Sometimes referred to as tele-research, the operator or a specialist agency undertakes targeted surveys to ascertain or obtain information about potential demand, reactions to campaigns, comments or service received.

> 'In any one week I attempt to make at least four telephone calls to obtain marketing information. Additionally, I send four hand-written notes to clients, and issue at least four sets of information – a "four"mula that works for me.'
> Source: Independent Hotelier.

Telephone research requires careful planning and targeting. Findings may provide the operator with useful market information in respect of individual demand, but are only indicators of general trends. For instance, an operator attempting to identify the demand for specialist conference business prior to expanding facilities may find that out of ten telephone calls only one respondent states any need for such a facility. Expressed in simplistic terms, if this response was mirrored through another 90 calls a market demand equating to 10 per cent of local business *may* have some need for such a facility.

A positive example of this is provided in Chapter 4, where approaches to marketing and sales by sector are discussed. This example illustrates how one specialist operator, Granada Studios, successfully utilises the above method.

There are, of course, other sources of research and information the operator could utilise. Telephone research provides a sample or snapshot of requirements or attitudes, and needs to be analysed alongside other data.

INDIVIDUAL OR PERSONAL INTERVIEWS

Many of the larger operators will utilise this method, usually attempting to identify either product awareness or perception. Canvassers or interviewers, usually employed by a specialist agency, will conduct a cross-section of home or street interviews with individuals. Pre-set questionnaires are designed and tested and the responses are collated to provide an overview. As with all questionnaires and interviews, there exist certain problems related to sample size, question training, respondent error, interviewer error and analysis. The polls conducted by various agencies during the 1992 General Election proved how wrong findings can be.

Operators, however, could conduct more in-depth interviews with existing or past customers, to obtain feedback on services provided and comments on future needs. Such a small sample could provide the operator with important marketing information, although again only in general terms.

MAILED QUESTIONNAIRE

The use of this method is increasing, questionnaires being sent to customers either with information about the operator's products or directly. There exists a range of skills required in the design, layout and content of questionnaires and basic guidelines are as follows:

- The questionnaire should have particular aims and focus on these.
- The questionnaire should be as short as possible, utilising either scales of preference or 'tick boxes' to speed completion.
- There is an advantage in offering some form of reward for completion, usually a discount off use of the operator's facilities or a small gift.
- Care should be taken to ensure language is appropriate, and is neither racist, sexist nor discriminating in any other way.

- The questionnaire should be titled clearly, and information and guidance should be provided on how it should be completed and returned.
- Assurances of confidentiality should be offered.

The normal response rate to questionnaires is fairly low. On two I completed recently, the first resulted in a response rate of over 82 per cent, while the second was 34 per cent. It is also important to analyse the quality of response and the appropriateness of informal received. Such questionnaires could be distributed to existing customers at appropriate times within the unit.

ANALYSIS OF INTERNAL DATA

The operator will (or should) have access to considerable historical data which, if collated and analysed, provides an invaluable source of related marketing information.

The problem with this is that information provided is based on *past* business, and will only provide indications on market trends to aid decision making. However, if research is carried out after particular promotional or sales campaigns, the operator will obtain direct information relating to the success of the activity and the actual return on revenue expended.

The sources of data are dependent upon the type of information the operator maintains. Additionally, the way in which data is kept will affect an operator's ability to access useful information. Such sources include:

- overall sales records;
- departmental sales records;
- customer details/guest histories;
- sales enquiries records;
- cost and revenue records.

As indicated previously, the computerisation of records is assisting the accessing and analysis of information.

ANALYSIS OF EXTERNAL DATA

There exists a considerable amount of marketing and market information obtainable from external sources. Government agencies, tourist and development agencies, specialist companies and media companies investigate and report on a wide range of subjects related to the hospitality industry. Such information may be the findings of highly targeted research or more general business or market reviews. Additionally, operators can purchase ready-made mailing lists for use within their own research.

Examples of external data include:

- the breakdown of readership for a magazine, newspaper or trade periodical;
- the results of a survey into accommodation take up;
- the results on research undertaken on consumers' attitudes towards forms of advertising;

- the reports from area tourist boards on occupancy rates and sources of business;
- the results of research on market demand for a particular product.

The type of data and analysis available is wide, and operators will need to be selective in both the analysis and utilisation of such marketing information. Operators require information that is relevant to their business and markets.

COMPETITOR ANALYSIS

The analysis of how competitors are performing can provide operators with indicators of either business potential within an area or the need for a particular product, or provide a form of evaluation of the actual business performance against others servicing a similar market.

Local trade associations and tourist boards provide details of local 'intelligence'. However, these tend to be centred on accommodation usage or overall visitor numbers. The information is often historical and, due to the competitive nature of the industry data, is often not obtainable.

Operators may conduct information surveys by visiting competitors' premises as a customer, and sampling service and products in an effort to identify both the competitors' strengths and weaknesses and to 'pick up' additional information. While a relatively crude research method, this can provide the operator with valuable information that will aid planning and decision making.

GUEST COMMENT DATA

Increasing numbers of operators will attempt to obtain feedback from customers through the use of a variety of guest comment cards or short questionnaires. As a method of research, this activity raises doubts. There exists a tendency for responses to be in the extreme, that is, very favourable or very unfavourable. As response rates are generally low, the sample can only provide general indications in respect of customer satisfaction or dissatisfaction. There also exist problems concerning the wording of such documents, and due to their nature they tend to be fairly short, concentrating on key elements of the business. Operators attempt a variety of approaches to solicit views from customers in written form, including comment cards left in bedrooms or attached to bills, comment cards left around the establishment for customers to complete *ad hoc*, invitations to suggest an employee of the month, mini-competitions or quizzes, and the guest comment book left by the cash register or reception desk.

In addition to the problems associated with their completion and the value of the information obtained, there is the question of how such 'feedback' should be utilised. Over a short period, I completed in detail eight comment cards and telephoned two units to express my thanks for the quality of service received. My aim was to ascertain how the information was dealt with, and while not a particularly sound piece of research, the results were as follows:

- Of the eight comment cards I completed with my name and address, I received two written responses. One response was a standard word-processed letter thanking me for my comments (in this particular case I had criticised aspects of the service). The second written response was more personalised, promised a form of review and expressed hope I would return again.
- In respect of the two positive telephone calls, the first was handled by a receptionist who thanked me for my comments. The second passed me to the general manager who identified for me the member of staff involved, thanked me for the information, took my name and address and followed the conversation up with a written letter. Needless to say, I am on the second unit's database now, but not that of the first.

To put this into a wider perspective, there is a need not only to obtain customer views to assist planning, but also to ensure that the information received is followed through and utilised effectively.

> Many operators make use of this technique to great effect: 'It may be a slight exaggeration to say our entire management policy is based upon guest comment cards. They are displayed in every bedroom and on all dining tables. A guest can enter bouquets or brickbats without the possible embarrassment of an ensuing conversation. The management team meet regularly to discuss those forms. Between 500 and 750 cards are reviewed each year. Analysis provides us with some important marketing information, for instance, reasons for the customer choosing our establishment, and sources of information, that is, guides.'
> Source: Eric Marsh, Proprietor, Cavendish Hotel, Derbyshire.

SUMMARY

The importance of identifying demand by systematic market research cannot be underestimated. Operators have available a variety of methods and sources of internal and external data. Market research appears a daunting task especially for smaller businesses, and it is true that certain of the methods require specialist skills and systems. However, the independent restauranteur, hotelier or licensee can undertake a variety of research which is neither costly or time consuming.

Having obtained the information, the operator is better placed to plan appropriately and make business decisions based on reasonable forecasts rather than pure guesswork.

The next section will look in more detail at the analysis and utilisation of market research information.

THE ANALYSIS OF MARKETING INFORMATION

Having recognised the importance of identifying customer needs and identified the various methods which operators can utilise, it is important to outline how the analysis of information forms the next important element in the process of managing the marketing function.

> The reasons for the careful analysis of information are easily recognisable in that:
> Incorrect interpretation could result in poor decision making, developing a potential loss of revenue, an increase in costs, the possible dissatisfaction of customers and the lowering of staff morale.

The role of analysis then is to:

- identify common factors that aid decision making;
- establish the validity of information in relation to a particular business or market;
- identify potential problem or risk areas;
- identify and evaluate market research methods in respect of cost effectiveness.

The analysis and evaluation of market research and information is crucial, and one that can include very detailed and time-consuming activities. Obviously, the larger and more complex the research and information, the greater the need for detailed analysis.

Such investigation is also linked to the cost elements and risk factors involved. The development and launching of a completely new range of themed restaurants or lodge-style hotels will possibly require years of research and investigation, coupled with detailed planning and testing, while the commencement of a diners' club for a hotel may involve the operator in only minimal analysis.

Whatever the scale of the analysis and potential activity, the key factor is to minimise risk by identifying demand in more precise terms.

THE BASIC METHODS OF ANALYSIS

STATISTICAL

Here the operator will analyse marketing data of various types and attempt to identify more precisely information that indicates potential trends, market demand and possible sources of business. Data and figures are cross referenced and reports produced with recommendations.

FIELD TESTING

Having obtained the information that appears to prove or indicate certain trends or preferences, further analysis will be undertaken to test the information. Existing customers may be utilised on pilot units and facilities set up. The operator then concentrates on establishing the true nature of demand and builds in the opportunity for adaptation of the product in light of users' comments.

EXTERNAL VERIFICATION

Some operators will employ specialist agencies to review information, provide additional analysis and recommendations.

In certain cases all three activities will be undertaken alongside other activities, again with the aim to ensure that the research has provided the operator with correct information on which to develop or alter facilities and products.

PROBLEMS ASSOCIATED WITH THE ANALYSIS OF MARKET INFORMATION

- The majority of information is historical, that is, based on facts possibly true at one time.
- The research may have omitted certain key factors, or external economic factors may occur that could not be, or were not, foreseen.
- Competitors may emerge, who having access to similar information 'beat' the operator to the market.
- The analysis may indicate and recommend a path of action unacceptable to the operator.
- The analysis is still only a mere scientific 'guesstimate'.

SUMMARY

The analysis of marketing information is an important part of the marketing and sales function and requires certain skills and knowledge. For some operators, such analysis is too costly both in respect of revenue and time.

However detailed the analysis, the operator will add extra dimensions and considerations, including forecasts of revenue and costs. Additionally, there is the need to ensure that demand can be matched by the appropriate level of provision. The final section in this chapter deals with these important aspects.

THE ROLE OF FORECASTING AND BUDGETING AND MATCHING DEMAND TO PRODUCTS

This section deals briefly with the aspects of forecasting, budgeting and matching demand to products. While essentially operational dimensions of any business, they are considerations in the complete process of marketing and sales. I have identified marketing as the management process responsible for identifying and satisfying customer needs profitably.

If a business is to be profitable, a key consideration is the planning and preparation for expected demand matched to the estimated profit and actual return from business activity. For marketing and sales activity to be truly effective, there must exist elements of analysis of expected return against actual return.

Preceeding sections within this chapter have identified the importance in obtaining appropriate market information and conducting effective analysis of such information. The aim is to produce information that is appropriate, can be utilised as an aid to decision making and will assist business performance. Information obtained, therefore, must provide indications of both the level of demand and the degree of potential profitability.

THE ROLE OF FORECASTING

The majority of hospitality operators are involved in forecasting, that is, estimating the levels of business related to certain products, facilities, services and units.

A chef may estimate the number of diners from a list of bookings, or estimate the level of demand for certain dishes. This would affect the number of items ordered and prepared, staff required and the estimation of time free within a period to complete other tasks.

In the same way, hospitality operators have to forecast the level of demand related to past experience, numbers of enquiries, and information obtained to set the facilities required.

On a larger scale, an operator may forecast that demand for a new product or facility will be sufficient to enable the company to progress its completion. This forecast would not only relate to the overall level of demand, but also to the type of demand, its geographical distribution and the potential frequency of demand.

However, forecasting is not an exact science and is, at best, a good guess based upon all the available information and the experience of the operator. Forecasting may relate to a particular event, a product, or a range of facilities and services. The forecast may indicate potential business for a fairly short period, or for a particular facility in the long term.

THE ROLE OF BUDGETING

Hospitality operators have to ensure that planned activities have been appropriately financed in relation to the estimated level of demand and return (or profit). Managers and owners will seek to obtain details of the estimated and actual flow of business and related revenue, thereby ensuring that expenditure does not exceed return. Budgets, that is, the level of expenditure related to a particular activity, may be set for:

- marketing research;
- promotional and sales activity;
- advertising;
- staffing;
- building costs;
- provisioning; and
- discounting.

Additionally, an operator may estimate that a particular marketing activity should provide a certain level of return, either at some form of breakeven point, where returns match expenditure, or that returns should exceed costs by a fixed percentage.

Financial or business forecasts may have provided the operator with further information related to the type and frequency of demand, and indicated types of business or activity that would be 'unprofitable'.

By forecasting, the operator has increased information on which to set budgets and estimate cash flow, and will be able to ensure that increased demand for a product or facility is matched by appropriate supply.

MATCHING DEMAND TO PRODUCTS

Effective marketing and sales activity may have generated increased or altered demand; it is now the responsibility of the operator to ensure that the demand is matched by the product. In the television comedy series, *Fawlty Towers*, which detailed the activities of an eccentric hotelier, this was identified in the episode entitled 'The Gourmet Evening'. Advertising the event resulted in only marginal demand, and despite furious activity on behalf of the luckless hotelier, even the small numbers of customers ended up with no food.

Of course, this parody took things to the extreme, yet many operators fail to match product availability to demand, and thereby affect future sales and business. Problems can occur if:

- The product, service or facility provided does not match the expectations of customers. This could include aspects of perceived poor quality and inaccurate description of the product by the operator.

- Provision has been set for products and facilities that are not generally required. This could occur if initial marketing and planning has been incorrect, or if external factors occur that alter market demand.
- The level of demand exceeds supply to the extent that customers remain unsatisfied. This could result in customers moving to other operators.

SUMMARY

The importance of effective forecasting and budgeting, and the matching of products to demand can then be identified. The detailed explanation of financial management techniques is outside the scope of this text. However, its relevance has and will be stressed throughout.

CHAPTER REVIEW

This chapter has concentrated on the importance of identifying customer needs and outlined introductions to the elements of market research analysis, forecasting and matching planned provision.

Market and marketing research is a complex area, which requires detailed understanding of the processes involved and the factors that effect positive outcomes. However, there are a variety of activities that can be effectively utilised by operators.

This chapter has set the scene for readers to look at the common marketing and sales activities. Readers may wish to return to this chapter, and the preceeding ones, when working on these other sections.

KEY POINTS

- Identifying customer needs is the first stage in effective marketing and sales.
- Appropriate market research can provide the operator with invaluable information on which to base decision making.
- Market information, while invaluable in aiding decision making, is not a guarantee of business success.
- There exist both external and internal sources of information that an operating business can utilise.
- Having obtained market information, the operator needs to be aware of the importance of correct analysis, otherwise problems may occur.
- Operators need to identify the most appropriate and cost effective methods for identifying need and evaluating and utilising such information.
- The role of forecasting demand in relation to revenue and costs is the operational side of marketing management.

QUESTIONS

- Explain the importance of identifying customer needs in relation to decision making.
- List the reasons why an operator may utilise market research.
- Outline the methods an operator could utilise to obtain market information prior to launching a new product or facility.
- Explain the advantages and disadvantages of market research conducted by mail.
- List and evaluate in order of relevance and importance the various sources of market information a hotelier may possess.
- Explain the importance of analysing marketing information effectively.
- Identify problems that could occur if an operator had failed to satisfy demand by the correct provision of products, services and facilities in relation to further business.

CHAPTER FOUR

MARKETING
AND SALES METHODS

INTRODUCTION

This chapter is concerned with marketing and sales methods utilised by hospitality operators to assist both the identification of customer needs and profitable sales. Certain related aspects are covered in more detail in other sections of this text including:

- identification of customer needs and demands and market research (see Chapter 3);
- aspects of in-house selling (see Chapter 6); and
- personal selling skills (see Chapter 5).

This chapter will concentrate on the identification of appropriate methods, planning and control of costs, and describe in more detail the specific aspects of particular activities and their relationship to general marketing and sales activity:

- advertising;
- sales literature;
- telephone sales;
- public relations;
- the use of technology and the media;
- the use of agencies and consortiums.

By studying this section, reviewing the key points and completing the suggested assignment or exercise, readers should be able to:

- Have an appreciation of the importance of planning and cost control.
- Identify appropriate methods for particular marketing and sales activity.
- Understand the various types of advertising available to the industry and identify appropriate advertising methods.
- Appreciate the importance of related sales literature.

- Understand the use of the telephone in respect of proactive and reactive selling.
- List the types of marketing technology available to the operator and understand how technology can assist effective marketing and sales activity.
- Understand the role of public relations in the promotion of a company or product.
- Explain the ways in which agencies and marketing consortiums assist companies in respect of their marketing and sales activities.

PLANNING, METHODS AND CONTROL

You will have identified that there exists a variety of marketing and sales methods and activities. The importance of identifying the most appropriate method or mix of methods is stressed throughout this book. Additionally, the need to plan both appropriately and control effectively are key primary considerations for individuals or organisations involved in marketing and sales activities.

While it is important to look in detail at these aspects, positive and effective marketing and sales is concerned in the end with *actions* and *outcomes*. Later sections within this chapter and sections within Chapters 6 and 7 will identify in more detail the types of common activity that, by their actions, assist positive outcomes.

The operator often has little time to consider the intricacies of various marketing theories and concepts, or to debate the 'morals' of various strategies. While they may be considerations, the emphasis is quite justifiably on ensuring the survival of the business. This holds true whether the business is within the commercial or welfare sector. Taken from this viewpoint, hospitality operators will need to consider the effective identification of methods and set up appropriate planning and control mechanisms.

Within Chapter 2, the role and function of marketing planning was described in detail, while in Chapter 3 the importance of this primary marketing function was outlined along with the various methods for achieving appropriate marketing information. This section will concentrate on the identification and range of the most commonly utilised methods or 'actions', and stress the importance of linking these actions to systems of control.

THE IDENTIFICATION OF METHODS OR MARKETING ACTIONS

As identified in Chapter 3, there exists a variety of methods for obtaining appropriate marketing information. It would be wrong to assume that such activities as market research, customer surveys and business analysis, are the only source of marketing information. The effective utilisation of a variety of marketing and sales methods or actions can also provide the operator with additional sales leads and opportunities. Therefore, the role and function of marketing and sales actions is not just to boost sales, or to promote a product or facility. By their effective completion, they can and do assist the operator in a variety of other ways.

It is important to outline the various methods or actions available to the operator before identifying the ways in which such actions are selected.

MARKETING AND SALES METHODS OR ACTIONS

Marketing and sales personnel often refer to the various methods in respect of how they interact with the consumer:

- *Indirect actions* refer to activities which, while they do not 'sell' a product, service or facility directly, assist this function by creating customer awareness or increasing availability and access. An example of indirect action would be PR (dealt with later in this chapter).
- *Direct actions* refer to activities which concentrate on closer contact with existing or potential customers. They are an outcome of research and promotion with the central aims of achieving sales. An example of direct action would be a sales presentation or a face-to-face selling situation. (This is described in Chapter 6.)

Backing up these two main groups or areas of actions is the concept of the four P's: product, pricing, promotion and place (which is described in Chapter 1).

While the differentiation between the two groups can become blurred, this separation will assist the operator in analysing the potential effectiveness of an action and the mechanisms of planning and control required.

INDIRECT MARKETING AND SALES ACTIONS
(SEE ALSO LATER SECTIONS IN THIS CHAPTER)

ADVERTISING
Advertising covers many forms and plays an increasingly important part in marketing and sales activity. A costly activity which requires special skills on behalf of the operator, advertising covers the majority of the senses in that it can be visual, that is, pictures and images, written or sound, as in radio. The majority of hospitality operators utilise advertising to some degree, and such advertising may be external, that is, delivered through some form of media, or internal, that is, displayed within an operator's premises.

Sales literature

The majority of operators utilise some form of sales literature to provide information about products and facilities and to promote the benefits attached to these services. While not often seen as a sales action, they can and do positively assist the operator and the customer.

Some operators may produce a wide range of glossy and expensive sales literature, while others may only be able to offer a minimum of material, for instance, the menu.

In the late seventies, a good example of 'menu selling' was conducted by the Bortsch'n'Tears restaurant in London. Its comical and amusing menu was widely displayed in London's underground system to great effect. Whatever the form sales literature takes and whatever the main purpose, effective sales literature performs important functions in both informing consumers and providing positive sales messages.

Public relations

Public relations is often described inaccurately as 'free publicity'. As you will see later in this chapter, the PR function is much more complex than that. Its role is to create improved understanding between a company and its customers and contribute positively in selling related products or services.

Sales promotions

Promotions are often aimed at creating existing or potential customer awareness of a product, event or special benefit. Certain promotional activities fall more easily into the direct selling category. However, due to the impersonality of the activity, I would consider them indirect actions. Effective promotions can assist the operator in a variety of ways.

The use of technology

Advances in communication and distribution technology have assisted operators in improving the access and availability of their products, services and facilities to an increasingly competitive and complex market. The capture of guest data provides the operator with important marketing information, allowing the targeting of other marketing and sales actions.

Customer care

The hospitality industry has moved away from a product-orientated marketing approach over the last decade to a consumer-orientated strategy. Effective customer care is recognised by many as being one of the key elements in developing and maintaining profitable business. Improved customer satisfaction will affect future sales and business.

Indirect marketing and sales actions can be seen as actions that, while not dealing directly or personally with potential or existing customers to affect additional sales, exert considerable influences on consumer buying behaviour.

DIRECT MARKETING AND SALES ACTIONS

FACE-TO-FACE SELLING

For individuals being introduced to marketing and sales, a common misconception is that activity is dominated by some form of 'car salesmanship'. Selling is often seen as a hard activity characterised by aggressive sales approaches. With a few exceptions, such an approach is very rare. Positive face-to-face selling is a common situation within the industry, and one that requires special skills, knowledge and attributes. It is an outcome of other types of sales actions, such as advertising or promotion. (See also Chapter 6.)

SALES PRESENTATIONS

Sales personnel are often required to present their 'case' for obtaining business. This may be to a group of decision makers or to an individual with specific responsibility for hospitality purchasing. As the aim is to capture business, such situations are rarely approached 'cold', that is, without prior preparation or contact. (See also Chapter 6.)

TELEPHONE SALES

It could be argued that actioning sales by telephone is impersonal and therefore, indirect. However, considerable amounts of sales are achieved by the effective use of this medium. While cold telephone sales rarely achieve success, the contribution such actions make to overall business should not be underestimated. (See also 'Telephone sales', below.)

AGENCIES AND CONSORTIUMS

Hospitality operators increasingly recognise the contribution booking agencies and marketing consortiums make to increasing sales. While they also assist indirectly by increasing channels of distribution, considerable amounts of business are achieved by the use of their services. (See also 'The use of agencies and consortiums', below.)

MERCHANDISING

Merchandising is the promotion of goods, services and facilities close to the point of sale. While elements of this sales action are impersonal, effective merchandising is concerned with direct additional sales. The use of this technique is increasing and is primarily aimed at increasing customer spend per head. (The importance of merchandising and its potential contribution to sales is covered in Chapter 7.)

Direct sales actions can be seen as activities in which hospitality personnel deal personally or directly with potential or existing customers and, therefore, require a particular range of skills and personal attributes.

SUMMARY

This loose grouping or identification of styles of actions provides the operator with indications of:

- the identification of appropriate actions;
- the planning and control mechanisms required;
- possible strategies for implementing actions; and
- the systems of evaluation required.

IDENTIFYING APPROPRIATE SALES ACTIONS

Having identified customer or market need, the operator will seek to select sales actions most likely to achieve the aims of the activity. The aims of sales actions may vary considerably from raising general awareness of a company, to targeting increased sales for a hotel's restaurant at weekends. Whatever the aim, the skilled operator will wish to concentrate effort on *actions that will generate positive results*. Therefore the primary considerations in selecting sales actions should be: are sales actions appropriate, both to the market targeted and to the company or organisation itself?

SALES ACTIONS CONSIDERATIONS FOR A MARKET

The selection should be checked against certain key questions:

- Will the sales action reach the targeted market in the most appropriate way?
- Will the sales action be likely to generate the positive results required?
- Is the type of sales action acceptable to the targeted market, in that the potential customers will understand and 'accept' the type of activity?
- Will the costs forecasted generate sufficient appropriate business? This factor is often the most difficult to estimate, but the easiest to evaluate.
- Do there exist the appropriate channels of distribution available for the planned activity?

SALES ACTIONS CONSIDERATIONS FOR OPERATORS

- What budget do they have available?
- What time constraints exist?
- Do they have the in-house expertise available or will they have to employ specialists?
- Does the sales action fit in with the overall strategy and the specific aims of the company?
- Does the type of sales action fit in with the style and goals of the organisation?

For operators who constantly utilise sales actions and have their own marketing and sales team, such questions cause only minor difficulty. For operators unused to utilising proactive methods, the selection will be more difficult, and without expert assistance such operators may find their first attempts result in poor returns.

Another recognisable characteristic is that organisations will concentrate on actions they recognise as low risk, hesitating to expend money or time on actions that they are unfamiliar with.

It is true that all sales actions possess an element of risk, and not all will work as planned. However, by considering carefully the factors identified above, operators that have utilised other marketing techniques, such as research, will increase their chances of success.

Having identified the type or types of sales action most likely to achieve this success, the operator then needs to both plan and control the activity.

Effective planning of sales actions

The importance of planning is stressed throughout this book and is a key part of marketing and sales activity. Sales actions also require effective planning, although not disproportionate to the expected outcomes or benefits. Planning should be related to achieving the expected outcomes and concentrate on the key aspects of:

- *Financial planning:* to ensure that costs are within budget and mechanisms set up for control.
- *Responsibility planning:* to ensure that individuals, groups or agencies understand clearly their particular roles.
- *Timing and target setting:* to identify when elements of the sales action will take place and what targets are expected.
- *Evaluation planning:* to identify appropriate evaluation mechanisms.

Such planning may cover a reasonably long time period for major activities or relate to a single event. For instance, an operator planning to utilise local advertising to promote a special function will want to ensure that the advertisement is appropriate; that it is placed in the correct media at the most effective time; that staff are briefed on how to respond to enquiries and bookings; and that results are recorded so that a true evaluation of the success of the sales action can take place. This introduces the last aspect of this process, that of control.

Controlling sales actions effectively

The aspect of control is one which operators often omit – due perhaps to the idea that all business generated from sales actions is appropriate. Even in times of serious recession, this may be far from the truth and operators constantly have to analyse their business mix to ensure the correct ratio or mix of customers.

In respect of controlling the sales action the operator should:

- Check that forecasted expenditure is not exceeded unless appropriate.
- Ensure that staff are responding to generated enquiries effectively.
- Check the ongoing results from actions, to identify whether any adaptation to activity is required.
- Conduct analysis of enquiries.

The degree of control will relate to the scale of the activity, and becomes increasingly complex for larger organisations. Without appropriate control, the operator will risk overrun of costs, inadequate response and the possible loss of other sales leads and opportunities. In respect of the type of business generated the operator should:

Analyse additional income against the cost of the activity – although there may be circumstances when low margins of return are acceptable.

Analyse the range or type of business generated. This aspect is of particular importance as the operator may discover that:

- Generated business was mainly from existing customers taking the opportunity to cash in on a discount scheme.
- Additional business is inappropriate to the organisation, that is, new customers may drive away existing ones.
- A high percentage of business is being generated from a particular source or area.
- The business is becoming over-reliant on a particular type of customer or market.
- That new customers provide an additional opportunity for further targeting.

Control then relates not only to aspects of costs, income and profits, but also to a range of analyses required to assist effective marketing and sales actions.

Summary

There exists a variety of marketing and sales methods or actions that the operator can utilise. Many are fairly standard and used extensively by organisations on a continuous basis as part of an overall marketing and sales strategy. For each method of action, there needs to be carefully considered aims and operators will need to plan and control such actions effectively.

ADVERTISING

The best form of selling is face-to-face – where the client and sales person can directly communicate. The sales person can then establish precise client requirements, and through careful negotiation satisfy these requirements.

However, due to the nature of the industry's products and services and the geographical spread of its potential clients, the hospitality operators have to make use of other selling devices. Advertising is a widely used method, and one on which vast amounts of revenue are expended annually. This section will concentrate on the basics of advertising methods and effectiveness related to the hospitality industry.

WHAT IS ADVERTISING?

Advertising is perhaps best described as the use of mass communication media to influence existing or potential customers' attitudes and behaviour towards a product or service. It can be separated from non-paid advertising, such as public relations or free publicity, by the very fact that it is sponsored and paid for by the company. Advertising then is the paid for selling of messages with a variety of forms and aims.

THE IMPORTANCE OF ADVERTISING TO THE HOSPITALITY INDUSTRY

Hospitality operators seek to provide products, services and facilities that consumers will wish to purchase. Consumers, however, will only purchase those goods and services of which they are aware and which they believe meet their needs. Therefore, operators will seek to both raise the awareness of their products, services and facilities in their target consumer groups and to encourage them to purchase. Advertising, despite its often high cost and other weaknesses, is an important element in attracting additional business and profit. At its best, it will be part of a package of marketing and sales measures designed to maximise profitability. At its worst, it is a high cost element which, if managed incorrectly, can cause serious problems for the operator.

Hospitality operators advertise to maintain and improve their business. The type of advertising will depend on a wide range of factors, such as budget, selling objectives and target audience.

THE COMMON STYLES OF HOSPITALITY ADVERTISING

Advertisements come in three basic forms or styles:

- *Informative advertisements:* designed to inform prospective clients about a product, service, facility and, by inference, the company's existence.
- *Persuasive advertisements:* designed to attract potential clients and influence them to purchase.
- *Conformative advertisements:* designed to maintain confidence in clients who have purchased.

Some advertisements will contain elements of all three forms or styles, and whatever the medium used the advertisement will have at least one of these aims as its base.

The role of these styles of advertising is to influence consumer attitudes and behaviour to achieve three main objectives:

- to raise awareness of the company;
- to increase sales for the company;
- to create an ongoing favourable image and confidence of the company.

To achieve these aims and objectives, the advertising must be planned carefully, and fully costed. It should follow the basic principles of advertising, be targeted and have some method of evaluating its success built in.

THE DESIGN AND CONTENT OF ADVERTISEMENTS

The design of advertisements is best left to professional advertising agencies. Poorly presented advertisements compiled by the enthusiastic amateur, while being considerably cheaper, will usually not achieve any of the objectives set.

While the design is best completed by others, it is useful for the hospitality operator to recognise what comprises a good advertisement. Its content and style will depend on whether it is for use on television, in newspapers, periodicals or magazines, on billboards or on radio.

Whatever the medium used, the basic guidelines for effective advertisements are:

- Have a clearly defined objective, that is, identify what is being sold.
- Sell only one product – selling too many confuses the audience.
- Keep the sales message simple.
- Tailor the advertisement to the target market.
- Measure the results of responses – how else will you know if the expenditure has been worthwhile?

- Ensure that the advertisement is legal and complies with the legislation for such material.

One simple measure of an advertisement is known as AIDA.

Attention: does the advertisement grab the audience's attention?
Interest: does the advertisement arouse interest in the audience?
Desire: does the advertisement create a desire in the audience to purchase?
Action: does the advertisement contain information that allows the audience to action their possible purchase?

THE PLANNING OF ADVERTISING CAMPAIGNS

Whatever the size of the campaign, the operator will need to plan effectively, gaining maximum benefit from the time and money spent. Again, large campaigns are often planned in conjunction with professional agencies.

Fig. 4.1

EXAMPLES OF SOME GOOD QUALITY NATIONAL ADVERTISING MATERIAL FROM FORTE HERITAGE AND EDWARDIAN HOTELS

However, the hospitality operator will want to:

- Set clear objectives for the campaign.
- Identify an appropriate budget and timescale.
- Identify target audiences.

Fig. 4.2
AN EXAMPLE OF LOCAL ADVERTISING, TAKING ADVANTAGE OF PEOPLE'S LOYALTY TO LOCAL NEWS ISSUES.
THIS ADVERT IS FROM THE CHESTERFIELD ADVERTISER

- Identify the message it wishes to convey.
- Identify the most effective media, location and timing for the campaign.
- Tie advertising in to the overall marketing plan.
- Ensure that some form of measure of success of the campaign is built in.

Having set clear objectives and identified targets, the operator will need to determine the most appropriate medium for the advertisements.

TYPES OF MEDIA

The selection of these will be dependent on a variety of factors, such as cost and budget, and target audience. Is it a local, regional or national campaign? Is it short-term advertising for a single product or event, or long-term advertising to raise general awareness?

Having clearly identified the objective, the choice of medium for the hospitality operator is wide. The limiting factors mentioned, such as budget and target audiences, will then assist in the identification of the most appropriate medium. All have advantages and disadvantages.

NEWSPAPER ADVERTISING

Advantages:

- There is good national, local or regional coverage.
- The cost per client reached is relatively low.
- The targeting of market segments or groups is reasonable.

Disadvantages:

- Short shelf life, that is, daily newspapers.
- The impact of the advertisement is often reduced by other advertisements.

MAGAZINES AND PERIODICALS

Advantages:

- Already targeted at particular market segments.
- Larger reading audience.
- Longer shelf life.

Disadvantages:

- The cost per client reached is relatively high.
- Infrequency of publication.
- The evaluation of the response is more difficult.

Radio advertising
Advantages:

- There is good local coverage.
- The audience hears the advertisement by itself.
- It is an excellent medium for encouraging a quick response.
- The cost per client reached is low.

Disadvantages:

- The targeting of market segments is difficult.
- A sound message only.

The three media above constitute the most commonly utilised by the hospitality industry. The others listed below are made use of less frequently.

Television advertising
Advantages:

- Regional segmentation.
- High impact visual messages.
- Mass communication.

Disadvantages:

- Extremely high cost.
- The targeting of market groups is difficult.

Outdoor advertising
Advantages:

- The cost per client is very low.
- High coverage
- There is an opportunity for dramatic, eye-catching advertisements.

Disadvantages:

- Insufficient targeting.
- A long response time.

Other media could include cinema and video advertising, directories and guides and, perhaps, company newsletters.

COSTS, CONTROL AND EVALUATION OF ADVERTISING

As with all other costs, the operator will need to cost advertising activities carefully. The expenditure for advertising must be accounted against forecasted revenue gain. Therefore, the operator will require some form of measure to evaluate the success from a particular advertisement or campaign.

> 'Too often in our industry, ads are created, media chosen and space booked without creating the necessary monitoring systems. If you don't monitor the results, on what basis can you decide whether or not to repeat the campaign again?'
> Source: Hugh Taylor, Edwardian Hotels.

With some forms of advertising, the evaluation of success is difficult to identify, especially where the advertisement is not designed for a single event or facility. Awareness-raising campaigns are a good example of this. However, the operators will want some measure of effectiveness – how else will they ensure the maximisation of benefit?

SUMMARY

Advertising is an important part of marketing and sales activity. The hospitality operator will need to utilise advertising in one form or another to create and maintain consumer awareness and to induce attitudinal and behavioural change. It is an activity that must be planned carefully, tying in with the overall marketing and sales plan.

Many operators are unable to advertise nationally or find such advertising produces only minimal business for the costs involved.

SALES LITERATURE

All hospitality operators use sales literature to raise greater awareness of their products and to encourage purchase or utilisation. Examples include direct mail, brochures, newsletters, catalogues, sales letters, information packs and annual reports.

It could be argued that other promotional items, such as stationery, notepads, diaries, calendars and pens, should fall into this category, too. Many hospitality operators will utilise these. However, they would not normally be classified as literature.

> DEFINITION OF SALES LITERATURE
> Whatever the type of hospitality unit the operator can and should make positive use of such material. As in all sales and marketing activities their use should not be undertaken without appropriate planning.

THE SEQUENCE OF PLANNING

- *Identify the purpose:* example or consideration. Is the material designed to create sales or create image? Often the problem is that sales literature attempts to do everything.
- *Identify the objective:* what is being sold again? Too often literature attempts to sell everything. Planners will often want to define a measurable objective.
- *Identify target audiences:* who are they? Where are they? Are they existing or prospective customers?
- *Consideration of constraints:* how much time and money are available?
- *Identify the format:* the selection of the most appropriate material or method.
- *Production:* the appropriate professional production of the literature.
- *Distribution checks:* how is the customer going to receive the literature and who will distribute it and when?
- *Evaluation:* the measurement of outcomes and returns against effort and costs expended.

Obviously, a national sales campaign involving direct mail and brochures will require considerably more planning than a targeted sales letter to local customers publicising a one-off event. However, the considerations are basically the same.

Sales literature, then, serves a variety of purposes, attempting to reach existing and potential customers. The examples provided above all have their own specific purposes, advantages and disadvantages. The operator has to decide the most appropriate to achieve the specific objectives of the campaign.

COMMON TYPES OF SALES LITERATURE

The most common types of literature are direct mail in the form of leaflets, letters and brochures.

DIRECT MAIL

This literature is printed sales material and letters sent directly to a company or individual. In wide use nowadays and utilised by many service-type industries and retailers, direct mail has distinct advantages over other methods if planned carefully. Its use is best when part of other marketing and sales activity, and

Fig. 4.3

DIRECT MAIL WITH A DIFFERENCE. THE BRIGHTLY COLOURED POSTCARD DRAWS OUR ATTENTION, THE
REVERSE SIDE GIVES THE TARIFF, AND THE ADDITIONAL MATERIAL SUPPLIED GIVES US MORE RELEVANT
INFORMATION

while it cannot replace more personalised forms of selling, it can reach potential customers in a relatively inexpensive way.

GUIDELINES FOR DIRECT MAIL MATERIAL

- The literature should be targeted carefully.
- The material and copy should be of a high standard, utilising if possible both pictures and text.
- The material should be laid out in a way to encourage reading, by the correct use of type, with positive, attention-grabbing headlines.
- The content should encourage the customer to buying action by outlining benefits and providing a choice of response devices.
- If possible, the letter should be addressed to an individual and, if the mailshot is a fairly small one, with the envelope handwritten.

Direct mail material may include brochures or leaflets, usually accompanied by a covering letter. Many companies utilise this type of material usually to targeted individuals or companies, whose details have either been 'captured' by previous use or obtained from a purchased list. Many companies sell such lists and will often produce specialised lists for a geographical area, or by type of business. However, the utilisation of direct mail has several disadvantages:

- *Inadequate targeting.* While you may have a name, that person may not know the organisation or have any experience of its services. There will be an in-built reluctance to pursue the offer unless it directly appeals to an immediate need.
- *Duplication.* Most individuals receive considerable amounts of unsolicited mail from a wide variety of 'sellers'. Given the increase of such mail and the perception of many individuals that it is a hard sell, take-up rates will be low.
- *Cost.* Costs may be high, especially if the material is in colour and professionally designed and printed.

SUMMARY

Direct mail is best utilised for highly targeted 'sales and promotional' drives and, while successful in certain circumstances, can create negative responses from regular recipients.

SALES LETTERS

Hospitality operators often utilise letters to promote facilities, events or services to both existing and potential customers. Cheaper to produce than complex direct mail material, letters are utilised in two basic ways:

- to promote a response; or
- to respond to enquiries.

PROMOTING A RESPONSE

Here the letter is being utilised to create awareness and promote the use of an event or facility. The key points for the use of such material are:

- Put a header in the letter. A header is a short sentence which describes in a few positive words the event, facility or service.
- Handwrite the individual's name – this creates a more personal style and image.
- Keep the 'copy' to one page – longer copy is not usually read.
- Keep sentences short and use a maximum of three to four paragraphs. Most recipients 'scan read', that is, they quickly peruse the page and do not usually read long copy.
- Ensure that the letter contains positive words. Known as 'power words' by copy writers, such words include: now, today, same, proven, results, discover, profit, benefit, trust, safe, you and your. The use of such words as our and ours create negative responses in the recipient.
- Ensure the copy explains clearly the product or event.
- Encourage 'response' – by including guidance of what the recipient should do now within the text.
- Sign the letter personally.
- End it with a postscript. The majority of recipients read this, although its use may appear as a hard sell. One way round this is to handwrite the postscript.

Sales letters should be carefully targeted and they are best utilised for past customers who have some experience of the company or unit. Additionally, the operator will want to identify whether the letter has generated a response, so some form of evaluation and checking system will be required.

As with all such materials, the timing of distribution is important and knowledge of purchase patterns or 'seasonability' of demand is an important consideration.

SUMMARY

With the advent of word processors and the facility to personalise letters, effective sales letters can be a useful aid to developing business. Usually the more personal the style, the higher the response rate. The costs of such material are fairly low, and personalised letters (and envelopes) are more likely to be opened and read.

However, due to the personalisation of the letter the information is likely to stay with the recipient and not be passed to colleagues (known as 'pass along' or 'pass through' by direct mail experts). Additionally, if the promotion is not of immediate interest, the letter is quickly discarded, in contrast to other sales literature, such as brochures or newsletters.

RESPONDING TO ENQUIRIES

Similar guidelines exist for sales response letters to those for sales promotion letters. Whether the customer has met the sales person face-to-face, made enquiries by telephone, fax or in writing, operators should ensure the following:

- A quick and efficient response to an enquiry.
- That the letter is well laid out, correctly spelt and that 'appropriate' language is used.
- The length of the letter is kept to a minimum, concentrating on the known information (or understanding of it).
- That the content, while professional, is neither too bland, for example, 'to confirm your reservation of . . . thank you'; nor too 'flowery', for example, 'Thank you for your kind enquiry and reservation for accommodation on the 12 January 1993. You can be assured that our staff will do everything in their power to ensure you have a happy and relaxing stay with us. During your stay you may wish to partake of meals in our restaurant, famous for its haute cuisine and fine wines . . .'

   The second example is an extract of a letter I received in response to a telephone enquiry and faxed confirmation!
- If possible, all response letters should be signed personally with a clear signature and job title.
- The letter should detail clearly the next action, for example, 'I look forward to meeting you'; 'If you would forward the deposit indicated above by . . .'; 'Upon receipt of your final numbers I will . . .'

Word-processing facilities speed up the time it takes to respond and also retains the personalised element of such communications.

SUMMARY

Sales letters, whether promotional or response type, should reflect the professional nature of the business and increasingly the aspect of positive customer care. In both situations, the letter forms part of a contract or understanding between the parties and, with careful planning and completion, can reduce the risk of misunderstanding or complaints.

BROCHURES

There exists considerable debate concerning the design, utilisation and effectiveness of brochures. Many operators will spend considerable amounts of money in creating such glossy literature. The cost-return factor is often not considered, and many operators see the brochure as a necessary evil.

THE PURPOSE OF BROCHURES

Brochures are usually designed to both inform and attract existing and potential customers. They usually concentrate on providing basic information, such as facilities, location and access, with accompanying images or copy to promote an image of the package of benefits to the customer. The range of brochures is considerable; they may be large packs of information, including a selection of material, or a simple two or three side leaflet. Many operators utilise a variety of more targeted brochures, in an effort to ensure the customer receives the appropriate information.

While the design of brochures is best left to the specialist, there are basic guidelines to their style, content and distribution.

STYLE AND CONTENT

The style of a brochure should be appropriate to the unit and the customer. A luxury five-star hotel will require a different style to a two-star hotel, and the contents will obviously depend on the type and range of facilities and services available. Styles include three-fold leaflets, book-type brochures, brochure packs where inserts can be altered, and single sheet leaflets (although this latter category is not really a brochure).

LAYOUT

Effective brochures will take a prospective customer through the various benefits, attempting to create a positive image of the unit, usually commencing with a brief description of the unit or facility, for example:

'A really luxurious country hotel amidst its own formal gardens and parkland' – Spa Hotel, Tunbridge Wells.

'Beautifully situated between towering Helvellyn and Ullswater in the centre of a small Lakeland village' – Glenridding Hotel, Ullswater.

'In the heart of theatreland, midway between the City and the West End' – Savoy Hotel, London.

'Beautifully situated in delightful gardens and commanding magnificent views across Falmouth Bay and the surrounding countryside' – Green Lawns Hotel, Falmouth.

'4-star luxury hotel superbly situated in the heart of Bristol' – Bristol Moat House Hotel.

Fig. 4.4
BROCHURES FROM THE DORCHESTER WITH THE ELEGANCE OF THE BROCHURE REFLECTING THE ELEGANCE OF THE HOTEL

Such descriptions are usually accompanied by a photograph or artistic impression of the unit. This introduces the unit to potential customers.

Following this initial attention-grabbing device are usually descriptions and images of the unit's facilities, products and services. A description of other facilities will follow and, finally, location, map and contact details. The trend nowadays is for the pricing structure or rates to be separate, usually on a single, half-size insert.

COPY

Captions to pictures and the main text should not be overdone, with over-elaborate details and claims of quality or value. While the copy should provide positive selling messages, the tendency of some operators to over extend copy is regrettable, for example:
'Dine in style, luxury and elegance in our sumptuous restaurant, find yourself pampered by our staff and enjoy haute cuisine and a range of connoisseur wines', or 'Memories to last a lifetime when you recapture the magic of romance'.

The copy should be precise, easy to understand, in an appropriate print style and reflect the benefits of utilisation (see Figure 4.5).

PHOTOGRAPHS AND IMAGES

Photographs or images, which clearly show positive aspects of the unit, work particularly well. Many hotel operators tend to use pictures of empty bedrooms, the hotel foyer or a deserted function room. It takes a skilled photographer to set and capture a selling image.

All images should be captioned, but not just with a description such as 'our standard bedroom' or 'the function suite', but rather a selling benefit, such as 'Excellent conference suites to ensure success for your business events'.

The provision of the necessary information is the base on which the brochure can become an effective selling tool. Operators will have to consider the cost and the distribution of such sales material.

DISTRIBUTION OF BROCHURES

Brochures are costly to produce and operators will obviously not want to waste revenue by a throw-away type distribution. Therefore, brochures should be:

- *Available and accessible to customers.* This might appear slightly nonsensical; however, many operators do hoard their brochures, appearing to be reluctant to distribute them.
- *Targeted.* It may be that a unit or company has a range of facilities and products, and they will require sales literature that promotes each one and reaches the appropriate person. (See Figure 4.6.)
- *Monitored.* If enquiries are received for brochures, the operator will want to receive feedback about the effectiveness of the material and follow up unfulfilled enquiries.

Corporate hospitality events in London, New York and Hollywood
(Available in Manchester City Centre.)

THE AA HITCH A RIDE THROUGH THE GALAXY

The Automobile Association business presentation began at 9.30 am with guests being ushered into the Art Deco splendour of the Baronial Hall for registration.

From the 1930's style cinema for the corporate film presentation their guests were then asked to fasten their seatbelts in MotionMaster - for some frighteningly reckless driving in a 15 billion dollar space ship.

Back down to earth, the elegant Victorian Foyer suite was the next venue for the final talk of the morning. Business concluded, but the entertainment far from over, their guests enjoyed a full backstage tour and a light cocktail buffet.

Selection of Wholemeal Cocktail Sandwiches

Fingers of Gala Pie

Marinated Melon and Pineapple

Celery Boats filled with Creamed Stilton

Hot Golden Turkey Cheese and Garlic filled Nuggets

Cod and Apricot Kebab

Mushroom Bouchées

(All served with Tea, Coffee and a selection of soft drinks)

BRITISH AIRWAYS HOLD THANKSGIVING DAY IN USA

The British Airways Executive Travellers' evening began appropriately in New York with our cast of characters saying a friendly 'hi there' to guests before they enjoyed a welcome drink.

After a BA video presentation in the 1930's style cinema, it was time for the flight that even surpassed Concorde: blasting through space and over a nuclear city in MotionMaster.

After a safe landing, guests were then escorted into the exhibition area before joining Black Rod and the BA sales team in the House of Commons debating chamber set for a presentation.

The Star Cloth Theatre was the ultimate venue of the evening, continuing the New York theme with an all-American Thanksgiving dinner created by our Head Chef, Peter Archer.

Fig. 4.5

COPY LINE FROM THE FRONT COVER OF A CORPORATE HOSPITALITY EVENT AND SOME CONTENTS FROM INSIDE THE BROCHURE

THE HILTON 8 HOUR CHAIR
We don't use dining chairs for meetings.
Instead, we have the Hilton 8 Hour Chair.
Tilt, swivel and adjust the height to suit
yourself, then settle down to business -
confident that your delegates won't be
finished before the meeting is.

**PROBLEM? NO PROBLEM -
WE CAN FIX IT**
You can count on us to fix things on the spot.
The projector bulb needs changing? No
problem. The slide tray has jammed? We'll
get it free.
If something goes wrong, we're ready.

YOUR BEST PRESENTATIONS
Your best presentations can be even better
in the Hilton Working Wall Room.
One simple remote control panel puts you
in command of an integrated audio visual
system, including TV, video, 35mm slide
projector and computer capability.
You'll find modern technology is made
beautifully simple.
Fully equipped for presentations and
training, each room is complete with
Hilton 8 Hour Chairs, hanging chart rails
and customised lighting.

DOWN TO DETAIL
When you have small working groups, we
have Break Out Rooms close by.
Each is equipped with comfortable chairs,
hardtop tables.

Fig. 4.6
TARGETED PROMOTIONAL MATERIAL WHICH HIGHLIGHTS PARTICULAR SERVICES AND FACILITIES AND
REACHES THE RIGHT AUDIENCE

Summary

The brochure is seen by some operators as a necessary evil, costly to produce in terms of both cost and time. Its contribution to sales is often underrated, and its distribution and effectiveness is seldom monitored. For certain sections of the market, the brochure will not affect buying behaviour. The group tour, or the business traveller, will purchase for a variety of other reasons. However, unless the unit is concentrating on one particular market, there remains the need for effective brochures to support other sales activities and material.

Flyers

These can be defined as one-sheet advertisements, usually concentrating on a particular event, service or facility. Depending on the style, the cost is less than

Fig. 4.7

A SELECTION OF CHEAP PROMOTIONAL
MATERIAL, FLYERS, BUSINESS CARDS AND MENUS

a complicated glossy brochure. While quite sophisticated 'flyers' can be produced incorporating colour images, usually such material is mainly text. Examples could include:

- cut-down versions of menus or the beverage list;
- details of seasonal functions, for example, Christmas;
- gourmet club details;
- description of special facilities, for example, leisure or conference suites;
- details of special weekend packages;
- details of a particular event.

Flyers should follow the same guidelines as other 'advertising' type material – concentrating on catching potential customers' attention, creating a desire to purchase and providing the relevant information to allow contact. The production of such material can be done in-house, given the appropriate

Fig. 4.8

HIGH QUALITY PROMOTIONAL MATERIAL FOR CAVENDISH HOTEL

facilities, or designed and printed by specialist firms. For chain operators there is a cost advantage when all units utilise the same material. Flyers can be displayed for easy access within the unit, enclosed in other sales literature or utilised in a targeted mailshot.

The last item of sales literature to include is the newsletter, an increasingly popular method, although not really direct sales material.

NEWSLETTERS

Company newsletters have been traditionally utilised in two ways, first, for distribution to employees and, secondly, for free distribution to guests. Naturally, the style and scope of the newsletter will depend on its target audience. Employee newsletters are dealt with in the section on public relations on page 129.

GUEST NEWSLETTERS

Many of the larger 'luxury' operators provide a glossy magazine-type newsletter, as do airlines and British Rail. Such magazines are designed both as a promotional device and as easy reading for 'captured' guests. The relatively high cost of such material is often offset by advertisements, and is usually only provided by the luxury operators. However, many smaller hospitality operators now produce forms of newsletter for existing and potential customers. With the advent of word-processing facilities and desktop publishing programs, quite effective promotional newsletters can be produced. For the production of such DIY newsletters, there are certain skills required and the copy has to inform readers of events and encourage increased utilisation.

The effect on sales of such material is often underestimated and even quite basic newsletters can produce reasonable response (if that is the aim of the material). One two-sided newsletter I produced resulted in 14 enquiries for a particular facility, and then seven firm bookings.

Very often, businesses will receive letters from companies announcing 'rather regretfully' price rises, or standard price lists. If these letters were turned into more positive selling messages, recipients may alter their buying behaviour considerably.

Targeted newsletters can indirectly or, in some cases, directly affect sales; regular customers may appreciate and enjoy receiving them, although they should not be too frequent. For a small hotel or restaurant, two to three times per year would be sufficient. Articles within the newsletter could include charity events, new menus, personalities making use of the premises and announcements of awards. The inclusion of articles about customers can be quite effective, as long as the operator has got their agreement for the use of their name.

SUMMARY

Newsletters can be a useful additional sales tool. Relatively inexpensive to produce and easy to target and utilise effectively, they form part of a company or unit's sales literature.

Before leaving this aspect of sales and promotion material, it is important to consider the types of promotional material often distributed free by operators or sold to guests.

PROMOTIONAL MATERIAL

Many operators provide such material for their guests. They generally fall into two categories:

- 'freebies', that is, material and items provided free for guests' comfort or utilisation; or
- merchandised material – items and products sold to guests.

Freebies are perhaps misnamed as the costs of such things as soap, toiletries, pencils and conference pads, have to be included in the price of the facility. Merchandised material has a more recognisable profit or return element, yet both, to varying degrees, assist the promotion of the unit or company. Such items are usually 'logo'd', that is, imprinted with the establishment's name and, better still, telephone number. Customers will often retain these for future use. I corrected the text for this book using a pencil printed with a hotel's name and telephone number, the diary on my desk was a gift from an establishment in the Midlands and I use daily a calculator provided as part of a conference pack!

Operators will use a variety of promotional material, including, increasingly, own brand items such as jams, sweets, drinking flasks and clothing. Their direct effect on sales may be minimal, but they do act as a re-enforcer of other more direct sales literature.

CONCLUSION

Hospitality operators make use of a variety of sales literature and promotional material to varying degrees of effectiveness. Well-designed, targeted sales letters and direct mail material are relatively low-cost methods for assisting sales, and they can be utilised by the majority of operators. Their advantage is their flexibility. Company or unit brochures do not usually possess this element of flexibility and their main function is to provide relevant information and positive selling messages. An operator will have to consider carefully the type, cost, range and distribution of sales and promotional material.

THE ROLE OF PUBLIC RELATIONS

'Positive public relations backed up by perfect sales literature, quality service and personal selling is of vital importance to every operator.'
Source: Eric Marsh, Proprietor, Cavendish Hotel, Derbyshire.

Public relations is an increasingly important part of the marketing and sales function, and provides the operator with positive support to sales and promotion activity. This section deals with the definition of PR, its contribution to effective sales activity, the specific role of PR, and common activities that are covered by this function.

PR is seen by some as a glamorous activity synonymous with entertaining and social events. In reality, effective public relations is an exacting business requiring particular skills often beyond the capabilities or experience of many operators.

While many of the larger companies within the industry either operate their own PR departments or employ specialists, PR is not limited to such organisations, and many smaller operators have made good use of PR to improve awareness of the unit and increase business.

This section deals with the growing importance of effective public relations, not only in relation to a company or operator's public image, but also how the positive use of PR can enhance other marketing and sales activities.

DEFINITION OF PR

'Public relations is the deliberate, planned and sustained effort to establish mutual understanding between an organisation and its public.'
Source: Institute of Public Relations.

This particular definition introduces several key factors. It identifies that PR is not a loose discipline based on glitzy production or unco-ordinated events, rather it is an outcome of effective, ongoing planning and implementation with an emphasis on developing positive contact with an organisation's public.

You may also wish to consider two other points of view on PR. The first is from Eric Marsh, proprietor of a highly successful hotel in Derbyshire. Mr Marsh has spoken to a wide variety of audiences on the subject of PR which he summarises as follows: 'PR is the result of generated goodwill, PR being the first two letters of PR-OFIT'. And 'There's only one thing worse than being talked about, that's *not* being talked about' – Oscar Wilde.

However you define PR, its role is to promote improved understanding between operators and their public. It is now important to look in more detail at the main functions and contributions of PR in relation to the hospitality industry.

THE CONTRIBUTION OF PR

The emergence of the specialist role of PR over the last few decades is one which has left many operators to reconsider the importance of such a function. However, forms of this customer understanding have been in existence within the industry for a considerable period. The famous hotelier, Cesar Ritz, and the master chef, Escoffier, both utilised PR to considerable effect in the early days of London's most famous hotels. By creating dishes named after celebrities of the day and encouraging patronage from the rich and famous, they not only 'pampered' their guests, but also generated considerable publicity for their establishments. While illustrating only one aspect of the function of PR, that of publicity, they certainly improved (at least initially) business. However, the contribution effective PR makes is much more than just publicity.

Eric Marsh, Proprietor of the Cavendish Hotel, has a particular approach to PR. He identifies the following team management practices which reflect his personalised, but highly successful, PR approach:
- go out and sell;
- emphasise benefits;
- greet guests personally;
- make guests feel important;
- put 'smile' notices on staff doors;
- provide real incentives for staff;
- innovate;
- set appropriate standards;
- promote and sell in a recession.

Increasingly, operators will utilise PR in a wide variety of ways, and while in one way it may be defined as 'free advertising', within today's complex market it plays an increasingly important part in creating image and customer awareness. For operators with limited marketing budgets, PR can be an effective tool for raising customer awareness.

'To enhance our restaurant's view of Chatsworth estate, we needed to move a telegraph pole from our grounds. I persuaded the Duke of Devonshire himself to "appear" to saw it down, and invited the media to attend. Even though the local TV station did not arrive until *after* the Duke had departed, they still devised a story and gave us two minutes' exposure in a regional TV magazine.'
Source: Eric Marsh, Proprietor, Cavendish Hotel, Derbyshire.

With larger operators, who by their nature and style are more separate from their customers, effective PR can assist in bridging the gap between the consumer and supplier.

Effective PR then contributes by raising the profile of a company to its public. It seeks to show a public face, one of concern, care and quality. While this contribution cannot be measured as effectively as other sales and marketing activity, its actual contribution to business may be immeasurable. In looking in more detail at the various functions of PR, it will be easier to identify some measure of this contribution.

THE ROLE AND FUNCTION OF PR

Operators will utilise PR for different reasons at different times. It has, however, two main functions:

- to solve problems; and
- to avoid problems.

In solving problems, the operator may utilise PR to create customer awareness of a new product or facility, to combat increased competition, to motivate sales personnel or to establish brand loyalty.

In avoiding problems, the operator may utilise PR to reinforce quality of a product against adverse publicity, to evaluate market demand or to create additional sales opportunities in a competitive market.

PR works in a proactive and, at times, reactive manner and is not just concerned with promotion. Realistically, PR is not concerned with direct selling, although the increase in sales may be the planned aim.

The PR representative may be involved in compiling press releases, organising a national product launch, dealing with adverse publicity, advising the management of potential problems, organising a photo opportunity for the press or preparing information for a company's employees or shareholders. Again, the role of such an individual will be dependent on the type of company or organisation. Additionally, many operators will employ specialist PR agencies to manage the PR function.

It is also important to recognise that effective PR should not just be concerned with external relations, a company's 'public' also includes its employees, shareholders and suppliers. In fact, anybody who may have an influence on its business. So its financiers, competitors and legislators could all be included to various degrees. Larger operators may utilise elements of PR in promoting its argument for favourable legislation, or promoting its contribution to environmental issues. Smaller operators may utilise PR in linking with local suppliers for promotional activity.

The growth in company newsletters over the past few years signifies the increasing importance of promoting the positive aspects of business to staff and shareholders, and is seen as a way of increasing the involvement of employees in PR activities (in addition to other aspects of effective human resource management).

Common PR functions and activities

Media relations

The media in all its forms plays an important part in assisting PR activities. The media obviously requires stories appropriate to the type of audience. This will involve the PR representative in:

- Creating an ongoing, professional relationship with the press.
- Providing information and stories by interview, photo opportunity or press release (this will be dealt with in more detail later in this section).
- Managing a press conference.
- Identifying appropriate media for developing stories.

Such a function will, similar to all PR activities, require effective management and particular skills are required.

Events

The industry is lucky in that it has considerable opportunities for events. The PR role is to ensure that they are managed correctly and receive the appropriate publicity. Events could include:

- the opening of a new hotel or facility;
- the arrival of a special customer;
- the launch of a unique weekend break;
- a member of staff winning an award;
- a major product launch;
- a major charity event;
- the announcement of a merger;
- a show or exhibition.

The list is endless and all operators have opportunities for such PR activity.

Without effective management and recognition of the indirect sales opportunities, efforts to increase awareness will be diluted. Additionally, the operator needs to be constantly identifying PR possibilities.

The primary purpose of PR then is to 'effectively support other sales and marketing activities attempting to build up a positive image of a company and its products and services'.

MANAGEMENT OF THE PR FUNCTION

Similar to other marketing and sales activities, PR has to be managed, that is, planned and controlled effectively, maximising on effort. Planning could relate to elements of a major product launch, a series of press releases concerning the opening of a facility or creating a photo opportunity for the local press. Control relates to the resources required and expended in relation to PR activity, and could include costs, employment and briefing of a PR agency, briefing of company personnel and setting up evaluation processes.

While smaller operators may only occasionally involve themselves in PR activity, effective management in such situations is just as important.

A STEP-BY-STEP APPROACH TO PR ACTIVITY

- *Establish the aims or objectives of the activity:* consider what is trying to be achieved.
- *Identify the methods and timing:* when launching a new hotel or menu, or opening a new facility, for example, consider what methods will promote the activity best and set appropriate timing for press releases, interviews, etc.
- *Plan the event:* ensure that resources, staff and facilities are prepared, including elements of costs.
- *Set responsibilities:* even for minor PR activities, ensure that staff are set responsibilities with appropriate briefing.
- *Ensure evaluation:* as with all marketing and sales activities, the identification of some form of evaluation or success measure is important.

By following a step-by-step approach, operators will be able to identify any possible problems and maximise on the sales opportunities created. Having looked at the elements of basic PR activity and the need for effective planned management, it is important to look in some detail at a few of the basic 'tools' of PR.

EFFECTIVE PRESS RELEASES AND RELATIONS

As already stated, part of the PR function is the development of positive relationships with the media. While individual operators or PR specialists may develop good personal contacts, they cannot hope to cover all possible outlets. The press requires copy, that is, stories that are interesting, topical and appropriate to their audience. The use of press releases is common practice, and a good way of creating additional interest in an event or activity. Additionally, they can be utilised to offset adverse publicity, although their use in such circumstances requires careful handling.

The press releases should:

- inform appropriate press of a newsworthy event;
- create additional interest in an activity;
- maintain contact with regular media outlets.

Press releases appear in various forms, and the content depends on the type of media at which they are aimed. They should contain as a minimum the following:

- a description or summary of the event;
- the date, time and location of the event (if appropriate);
- a brief outline of the 'story';
- the name, address and telephone number of the contact at the organisation.

They should also contain wherever possible some unique element, that is, one that is newsworthy and topical. For instance, the opening of a restaurant is not newsworthy in itself. However, if it is being opened by a celebrity or in unusual circumstances, its newsworthiness increases. Many operators will utilise such techniques to attract interest and, hopefully, increase positive media coverage.

The majority of press releases will concentrate on the basic points of *what, why, when* and *how,* leaving the media to write the article or story. With specialist trade journals and some elements of the national press, more detailed releases may be appropriate. Local papers, especially those that are distributed free, are often grateful for more detailed releases. However, the compiler of the release then has to possess appropriate skills in preparing copy.

Not all stories will be utilised and operators, especially those with smaller premises, will often give up after a few attempts. However, continuous use of press releases targeted effectively will reap rewards in the end.

Skilled PR operators will:

- develop and main relationships with their key media contacts;
- identify the type of story that will attract attention;
- ensure a reasonable supply of appropriate information to the media;
- target their press releases, improving the chances of utilisation.

Look at the articles printed in various magazines, newspapers and journals and consider that someone has had to put on the event and provide the information. Certain papers will have certain styles or audiences, they may also have identified feature writers or special sections that concentrate on particular aspects of news. Such analysis will indicate where and how news and information can be targeted.

Unique selling points

Marketing and sales personnel often talk of 'USPs' or the 'unique selling points' of an activity, event, facility or service. From the publicity and promotional viewpoint, a USP is something that attracts special interest to an event, or creates a positive image in the customer eyes.

USPs could include hamsters on the menu (tried by one famous hotelier), celebrity patronage, the luxury of a facility, the environmentally friendly aspect of a facility, the unique location of a hotel, the range of whiskies in a bar, or the fact that customers could act out being MPs, as in part of the Granada Studios facility.

Experienced operators will quickly identify that by utilising an effective USP, the possibility of positive interest is increased. Reference will be made to the use of USPs within the section on promotional events.

Summary

PR play an increasingly important part in the sales and marketing function. While it cannot be described as direct selling, its effective planned use can positively affect sales by increasing customer awareness. However, it requires appropriate planning and should not be aimed at simply seeking publicity. PR has an important role in providing relevant information about a company to its customers, suppliers and employees. Increasingly, operators need to understand or 'be close' to their customers, and PR performs a vital function in this respect by creating opportunities for the receiving of information back from the customer. While for many of the larger operators this function is handled by specialists, the smaller hospitality operator can and does utilise PR. The PR function requires certain basic skills. However, hospitality operators, by the nature of their work, possess ideal opportunities for indirectly increasing sales by its effective use.

The next section in this chapter outlines a direct sales method that has attracted a lot of interest over the past few years, that of the use of the telephone in promoting sales and reacting to sales opportunities.

Telephone selling

The use of the telephone by hospitality operators in responding positively to sales enquiries and developing sales has increased considerably over the past few years. Once frowned upon as a sales technique, hospitality operators have recognised that with careful planning and training, use of the telephone can be a very cost-effective tool for maintaining and increasing sales.

> Carys Thomas specialises in telephone sales training and has worked for many of the UK's top hotel groups. 'There exist two aspects of telephone sales, first, proactive telephone research when experienced sales staff attempt to identify potential contacts, business and sales opportunities, and, secondly, reactive telephone sales when staff deal with incoming enquiries.'

This section deals with how hospitality operators utilise the telephone in developing sales. Telephone technology is advancing and we may see more flexible and personal telephone reservation and sales systems in the future.

CENTRAL RESERVATIONS

Many of the larger hotel groups utilise a centralised reservation system. For the price of a local call, prospective clients can contact operators who can quickly provide information and book accommodation and facilities. This is possible for both national and international advance reservations.

A visit to such an establishment will leave the visitor considerably impressed with the speed and efficiency of response. Such a facility provides not only improved customer service, but reduces costs for the company.

Additionally, independent operators often utilise booking agents or consortiums to handle some of their telephone bookings. While this is not a proper selling activity, it does help increase sales by its availability and ease of use.

TELEPHONE RESEARCH

This is widely utilised by other industries and hospitality operators use the method in a variety of ways. Telephone research is used to identify particular company and individual needs, and establish sales leads and opportunities. Such activity is either carried out by designated sales staff, or subcontracted to a professional agency. As with all telephone sales activity, careful planning is required with specific objectives in mind.

As indicated, telephone research can be a very cost-effective method for obtaining information about a particular company or client. Irene Holdsworth, Swallow Hotels' Regional Sales Executive, outlines her approach to such important activity: 'Initial research of a company and analysis of potential business is of vital importance to developing business.'

Sales staff in such situations will often utilise a checklist identifying the key points they are attempting to establish.

> Irene Holdsworth advises:
> 'It is essential that a company obtain such information, because without it you are unable to establish what business opportunities may exist and then how best to take advantage of the sales opportunity.
> 'Effective telephone research is the first stage in capturing business – it lays the ground work for the salesperson to develop a positive relationship with the client.
> 'The most effective way of initiating and conducting such research is simply a well thought out and professionally undertaken telephone call.'

An example of such research could involve contacting a number of companies to ascertain:

- accommodation requirements;
- the type of accommodation and its location;
- the time of year and frequency of requirement;
- the individual responsible for making bookings.

Further details may be sought, including conference and training facilities and special events.

This information is recorded on a contact form or card, or entered directly on to a computer database as information is obtained. The information is then passed on to the most appropriate hospitality unit, regional office or individual to follow up.

While this method can be very cost effective in obtaining sales leads, as with all selling methods, it requires particular skills on behalf of the salesperson or researcher. It is a method often utilised prior to the opening of a unit to assist the creation of sales opportunities within a specific area or region.

TELEPHONE SALES

> 'Telephone selling is an extremely cost-effective method of identifying market information and all establishments should be involved in such activity.'
> Source: C Thomas, Telephone Sales Trainer.

It is sometimes difficult for individuals to differentiate between telephone research and telephone sales. Perhaps the easiest way is to identify the reason behind the call. Telephone selling is usually concerned with following-up sales leads generated by telephone research, response to advertising and written enquiries. The activity is designed to capture a sale by obtaining information from the prospective customer.

'Five steps to selling by telephone:

- sound customer and product knowledge;
- positive questioning technique;
- packaging the price;
- asking for the business;
- the importance of follow-up letter and information.'

Source: C Thomas, Telephone Sales Trainer.

Primarily, then, telephone research is concerned with identifying customers and their requirements, while telephone selling is concerned with more detailed activity designed to obtain business. Often one telephone call will not be sufficient to close a sale, unless other work has been completed.

Outline of the basic method

Whatever the situation, the salesperson needs to complete the necessary preparation before making contact by telephone. Considerable research has been completed on the right way to sell by telephone. Successful telephone selling is a skill gaining considerable recognition.

- Salespersons should be in an appropriate location, where they are unlikely to be disturbed.
- The information about the company or individual should be at hand, with a note pad and pen ready to take down details.
- As with all such methods, there should be an aim in mind. To obtain the business, confirm the booking, invite the prospective client in to view the facilities or arrange a personal call.
- The salesperson should not be drinking or smoking during the call.
- The message the salesperson is attempting to convey is one of interest and care about the client.
- The telephone conversation should not be too long, sufficient to get the message across, obtain information and identify the next stage.
- The timing of the call is important, but often a salesperson is not aware of the best time. If the customer is busy, an arrangement to call back is made.
- Politeness is of vital importance, and when starting the call and finishing, a smile and a sincere 'thank you' help to create the right impression.
- All telephone calls should be followed up by letter confirming details and the agreed outcome.

Both telephone research and telephone selling are types of outgoing calls, that is, calls made by salespersons to prospective clients. Both methods are becoming increasingly utilised by hospitality operators. However, the way in which incoming calls are dealt with is just as important, and one on which hospitality operators are spending both time and money in improving.

In-coming telephone calls

Excluding the central reservation facility, where staff are employed to concentrate on dealing quickly and efficiently with enquiries, in-coming calls to the hospitality unit require both efficient procedures and particular skills.

Incoming telephone calls cover a wide range of enquiries, and as it may be the first real contact a prospective client has with an establishment, it is important that all calls are dealt with correctly.

It is now common that the majority of calls are greeted with the name of the establishment and the name of the person receiving the call. In your opinion, which of the following responses is the best?

'Good morning/good afternoon. Thank you for calling the Excelsior Hotel and Conference Centre. Amanda speaking. Can I help you?'

'Good morning/good afternoon, Excelsior Hotel.'

'Excelsior Hotel.'

'Good morning/afternoon, The Excelsior Hotel. Can I help you?'

'Hello.'

Some are too long, two are too abrupt. The choice is really up to the hospitality operator. However, the response should always be the same with the right emphasis on a friendly approach.

Some guidelines on in-coming calls

The initial response:

- The telephone line should always be staffed during business hours. An answerphone is acceptable only in extreme circumstances.
- The response should always be the same.

  The second stage:

- The caller may require a particular individual or department. If that is the case, then they should be connected, without asking the enquirer for his or her name. If the individual is not available, the telephonist should politely ask for contact details and arrange for the individual to call them back (unless, of course, someone else could assist).
- If the enquiry is a general one, the telephonist may obtain details, or pass the person on to the appropriate individual.
- Whatever the outcome, the caller should be thanked and a confirmation made of the next action.

Some hospitality operators utilise notices close to telephones such as: 'remember to smile'; 'have you got the details'; 'remember to sell positively'.

> 'All staff have a key impact on sales, so all staff within a unit should receive training in telephone skills. Every telephone enquiry is a potential sale.'
> Source: C Thomas, Telephone Sales Trainer.

OBTAINING A SALE BY TELEPHONE

The skills of selling by telephone are in part similar to those utilised in face-to-face selling. The staged approach of operating, developing and closing a sale can be made use of to reasonable effect by telephone (see Chapter 5, 'Stages of the selling process').

CONCLUSION

The telephone plays an important part in marketing and sales activity. It can be used to obtain market information, identify contacts and sales opportunities. Additionally, professionally handled in-coming calls assist the creation of the right image. Telephones are a low-technology (at least in today's terms), cost-effective tool in both increasing and maintaining business.

THE USE OF TECHNOLOGY AND OTHER MEDIA

Hospitality operators have not been slow in recognising the part technology can play in assisting effective marketing and sales. Computerised reservation systems, account handling and data capture are increasingly utilised throughout the industry. The reduction in costs for such technology, its availability and adaptability have provided even the small operator with the facilities to maximise sales potential.

Electronic point of sale technology (Epos) including handheld portables (Cpos), are assisting in-house selling, while the use of electronic mail and selling by facsimile is increasing.

Operators are also beginning to utilise in-house television and video, and electronic display facilities to advertise and promote particular products, services, facilities and events. The use of electronic check-out systems has been tested at a number of hotels.

There exist many other examples of the use of more advanced technology within the industry; this section will concentrate on those that in my opinion are, or are likely to assist directly, marketing and sales activities. These I would indicate as follows:

- Computerised reservation and booking systems.
- Integrated computer systems that provide the operator with data on costs and yield, and information on guests.
- Account billing, especially when a customer data capture programme is integrated.
- In-house selling technology.
- The use of video or in-house television, both in promotion and for information provision.
- Word-processing facilities.

'The industry has not been particularly effective at positive marketing and sales and the assistance available from certain systems has been under utilised.'
Source: A Coby, Systems Consultant to the Industry.

Critics of some of the systems identified point to the depersonalisation of traditional areas of service, and it may be that for certain sectors of the industry, the use of technology may be inappropriate. Individuals utilising a particular French hotel chain, where check in, payment and room access is totally controlled by an individual's credit card, may also just as readily accept the efficiency and cost reduction.

Hospitality operators will seek to identify the costs of installing and making use of such technology against the benefits to the customer and the company.

'Appropriate cost-effective systems are available and can provide the operator with important marketing information. The vital factor concerns the way in which data is entered into the system.'
Source: A Coby, Systems Consultant to the Industry.

Technology in various forms can and does assist hospitality operators and their customers in a variety of ways. The marketing and sales function has been slower than some other aspects of the industry to utilise such technology. However, this situation is rapidly changing, which will become more apparent as you study details outlined below.

INTEGRATED COMPUTER SYSTEMS

The use of computers for invoicing, account handling and general 'back-of-house' functions has been fairly standard for a number of years. At first, computers were either huge, head-office mainframes or desktop systems. Advances in technology have provided less expensive and more reliable hardware and software, with operators setting up computerised links between units. Larger operators are increasingly investing considerable sums in such linking, for instance: 'Sheraton hotels reportedly invested $14 million (about £8 million) in improving its system to link all its international hotels': source: *Caterer and Hotelkeeper*, February 1992. The new Lansbury Hotel, London, has also invested heavily in integrated systems.

The purpose of such systems is to provide the operator with a wide variety of management information, which not only reports on actual business, but also can provide analysis of forecasted business and identify potential business.

> 'The ability to interrogate the system in order to obtain appropriate business and customer analysis is what operators should be seeking.'
> Source: A Coby, Systems Consultant to the Industry.

Integrated systems are developing fast, and include property and yield management programmes. Such programmes provide not only accurate reports on all aspects of the business linked to the main computer, but also important marketing information.

Companies, such as IBM, Welcome Hotel Computer Systems, International Guest Systems, Innsite, HIS and Logistrix, specialise in hotel computer systems, and many point to the increase in the use of property management systems (PMS). Entry level costs at present for a PMS system are a minimum of £6,000 to £7,000. Therefore, the cost benefit must be clearly identified in addition to the cost of possible breakdown or loss of data.

PROPERTY MANAGEMENT SYSTEMS

These aim to provide the operator with:

- centralised reservations,
- a computerised account system,
- revenue and costs accounting, reporting and analysis and, specifically, data on customers, which is appropriate for targeting mailshots, discounting and other marketing and sales activities.

YIELD MANAGEMENT SYSTEMS

These aim to provide additional information on accurate reporting of forecasted revenue, especially in connection with marketing and sales activities. Both systems, along with other packages, provide for the operator:

- an increase in marketing information;
- accurate analysis and reporting on costs and revenue;
- increased efficiency;
- improved customer service and benefits;

all of which indirectly assist the identification and satisfaction of customer needs.

The trend in systems, especially from the larger operator, will be towards PMS. The trend is really an adaptation of front-office systems with the possibility of improved integration.

COMPUTERISED RESERVATION SYSTEMS

Of obvious benefit to operators providing accommodation or conference facilities, such systems provide:

- increased customer access;
- increased channels of distribution;
- widening of the potential customer base;
- improved customer service;
- improved customer account handling;
- customer data capture.

While such systems are traditionally seen as more appropriate for larger hotel groups, the development of improved mini packages makes such technology well within the scope of smaller hotels.

Smaller operators, particularly those offering accommodation, require a basic system which allows the capture and utilisation of information such as sources of booking, geographical location, occupancy level and repeat business. The targeting of sales activity can then be undertaken.

IN-HOUSE SELLING TECHNOLOGY

The use of electronic tills is now commonplace throughout industry and hardware which provides end of day totalling, by product and by employee, are also widely utilised. Commonly referred to as Epos, such technology has improved financial accounting, security and customer service. Cpos equipment now allows the taking of orders electronically at the table or point of service. Linked by radio or infrared wavebands, such technology allows orders to be quickly taken and transmitted. An additional facility is for appropriate selling prompts to be displayed to the employee. For instance, during a morning period the order for coffee would prompt a message 'order for Danish', likewise in an evening period messages could include prompts for desserts, extra coffee or liqueurs.

While such technology is more appropriate for certain styles of operations, it does help to increase the average spend per head and improve customer care. Potential improvements are to link such technology to revenue and stock control, indirectly assisting operators in decision making.

WORD PROCESSING FACILITIES

Reasonably priced word processors have been available for some time and are in wide use throughout the industry. The humble word processor can (with the right software) perform a multitude of tasks which improve marketing and sales activity. (The research for this book was recorded on a word processor: the initial script was typed in, the numerous letters required produced and stored for reference and standard letters were produced which could be adapted quickly if necessary.) An enhanced word-processing facility linked to other computer software has the following advantages:

- quick, efficient, professional and personalised written responses to enquiries;
- storage of standard response letters;
- spell-check facilities and translation packages;
- storage of communications with customers;
- mailmerge facilities, allowing a personalised letter to be sent to a selection of identified potential customers;
- creation of more 'artistic' letters, posters, menus, and newsletters. The linking of word-processing facilities to desktop design packages is now relatively inexpensive, and the availability of colour printers provide additional opportunities for creative, low-cost sales material;
- creation of basic customer data or guest histories.

This type of technology is especially appropriate for the smaller operator.

VIDEO AND IN-HOUSE TELEVISION SYSTEMS

The use of such technology is increasing daily throughout many industries – main post offices have wall-mounted videos, slide machines and electronic sales displays, for example. For the majority of operators offering accommodation, the provision of in-room entertainment via the television is commonplace. The use of the in-room television as a vehicle for selling is just starting to be explored. Commonplace now are messages referring to basic hotel services, welcome messages and the provision of local information. In the future, subtle selling messages related to in-house provision, and other units within a company's portfolio will increase. Although a soft selling activity, and one which is rather impersonal for certain types of operation, such methods may increase sales considerably.

PROMOTIONAL VIDEOS

The use of short promotional videos has increased alongside other media technology. The costs of utilising such a medium can be prohibitively expensive with the price for a basic five-minute stills video starting at around £1,000.

Videos can be used to aid sales presentations, to send to individual customers requesting information and to promote companies to other distributors, such as travel agents and tour operators. Many of the larger hotel groups and tourist facility operators have utilised this medium, especially for the overseas market.

The video itself must be professionally produced and, similar to all marketing and sales activities, be carefully planned and targeted with specific aims identified. While their potential is often overstated, they do project a professional image (if prepared correctly), and provide customers with a strong selling message. Their use is often to complement other more personal sales activities.

There may be developments in the future connected with types of interactive video, where the potential customer is encouraged to participate in response activity. British Airways' use of innovative interaction via a cinema screen advertisement, prompted national press coverage in the later part of 1991. The advertisement included live participation by an 'actress' within the audience. Designed to promote bargain city breaks, the advertisement broke new ground which others may quickly follow.

CONCLUSION

The competitive aspect of the present and future hospitality market creates pressure on operators to undertake increasingly sophisticated marketing and sales activity. The concept of a global village, with rapid communications systems, indicate that various types of technology will increasingly be utilised to assist business survival. Technology which is readily available nowadays provides operators in all of the hospitality sectors with the means, albeit at a cost, to improve efficiency and maximise sales.

The next section in this chapter will look at the growth in use of agencies and marketing consortiums, a reflection of increased competitiveness within the industry.

THE USE OF AGENCIES AND CONSORTIUMS

Within Chapter 2, the concept of channels of distribution was introduced. It was identified that the industry is utilising additional channels to create improved customer awareness of, and access to, its products. It is important to deal with this aspect in more detail, identifying and illustrating how agencies and marketing consortiums assist both the customer and the companies' marketing and sales activities.

Agencies and consortiums charge fees or commission on business

generated, and the operator needs to analyse the cost-benefits equations of participation or membership. The competitive business environment supports the view that operators, especially in the areas of accommodation and facility provision, will rely more and more on such bodies in the future.

MARKETING CONSORTIUMS

The number of marketing consortiums has increased steadily over the past decade, and accompanied with this growth has been the specialisation of such organisations. In general, consortiums seek to attract members who offer certain standards and facilities similar to their existing members.

Consortiums act as brokers for the members, providing a range of services and sales and marketing assistance (at a cost). Typically, a consortium will charge a joining fee plus an annual subscription or membership fee. The annual subscription is often calculated as an annual charge per room. Charges may be made for additional services, bookings, brochure inclusion or specialist sales literature. Consortiums will often have predefined membership standards, including external inspection of potential properties and members. The members will benefit by:

- enlarging their potential market;
- having access to a centralised reservation facility;
- obtaining additional referral business from other consortium members;
- access to other groups and tour operators;
- representation overseas or at specialist travel or conference trade exhibitions.

Many of the consortiums operate types of 'clubs' for their customers, with facilities for centralised reservation, reservation guarantee, accommodation upgrading and a range of discounts. Such customer services are designed to create brand loyalty, encouraging regular customers to utilise operators from within the group.

Consort Hotels is one such consortium with over 220 members throughout Britain, whose stated purpose is 'to promote the facilities of its member hotels through national and international sales and marketing activities'.

'Consort Hotels offer a range of assistance to the members including:

- a commercial sales programme targeted at consort club members;
- facilities for central reservations;
- promotion of conference and banqueting facilities;
- targeted brochures;
- UK holiday brochure;
- group sales facilities.

'Additionally, other types of business and technical assistance are available, including speciality brochures, mailshots, PR, representation at trade events and exhibitions, and overseas representation. Such assistance provides the operators with marketing and sales support in areas which they could not undertake themselves.'
Source: Sue Tweed, Public Relations Officer, Consort Hotels Ltd.

Other agencies include Expotel, Bookatel, Pride of Britain, Preferred Hotels and Resorts, which covers luxury independent hotels world wide and includes hotels such as The Dorchester, The Lanesborough and The Ritz among its UK members, Leading Hotels of the World which includes the Savoy Hotel, and Best Western, which covers independent hotels in the mid-spend range. (My apologies to the consortiums I have omitted.)

Professional, well-established marketing consortiums approach marketing and sales activities in a similar way to large hotel groups, and provide members with positive business assistance.

While many of the operators who belong to marketing consortiums welcome the additional business and assistance, it must also be recognised that many (in the hope of an ideal world) would prefer to manage without them. Disadvantages are identified as:

- over-reliance on agency or consortium business;
- disagreements concerning commission rates;
- the depersonalisation of bookings.

The operator will need to identify clearly the cost benefits of joining a consortium, of which there are many. Detailed, continuous analysis of the

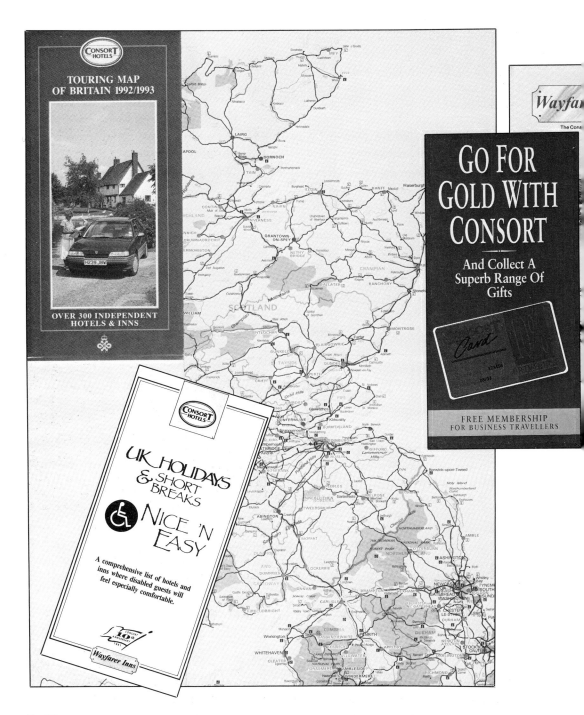

Fig. 4.9

PROMOTIONAL MATERIAL FOR CONSORT HOTELS CONSORTIUM. NOTE THE FREE MAP, A USEFUL AND
EFFECTIVE PIECE OF PROMOTIONAL MATERIAL

sources of bookings will provide the operator with a measure of the direct cost and revenue advantages of membership and, taken alongside the other services such consortiums offer, will identify the overall contributions membership provides. Additionally, the associated benefits to the customer should not be ignored.

BOOKING AGENCIES

Similar to marketing consortiums, a wide range of agencies exist including, The Modern Group who operate Expotel, The Peter Reid Group, Bookatel, travel agents such as Hogg Robinson, and major credit card companies such as American Express. These agents and others are in the business of accommodation and facility booking, and negotiate commission rates directly with the operators.

With turnover in millions and representing many thousands of bookings, agencies are not a factor to be ignored. On the positive side, they develop and channel considerable amounts of business to operators, and provide one-stop 'shopping' for independent and group customers. However, their position is seen by some in the industry to be too powerful, especially in times of recession. This attitude differs to other national markets, for instance in the USA where the use of booking agencies is widespread.

Many of the agencies in the UK provide other types of support for the industry.

> 'American Express, for instance, provides this type of support with a variety of initiatives.
> 'Such support has become increasingly sophisticated and includes such activities as advertising campaigns, direct marketing programmes, promotional magazines, competitions and trade shows. Hotel and restaurant guides are produced in conjunction with other international organisations and tourist authorities.
> 'Marketing partnerships like this provide prospective clients with a wider range of products, services and facilities. Additionally, it creates an improved image of the industry and its establishments.'
> Source: Sue Dorman, Public Relations Officer, American Express Europe.

The hospitality industry benefits overall from the activities undertaken by the majority of booking agencies. Again similar to marketing consortiums, agencies specialise in particular markets and this also assists the operator. For instance, convention bureaux or venue agencies may be able to attract more customers than an independent operator. Specialist tourist agencies will be able to target particular international markets out of the reach of many operators, while independent agents working in particular areas will possess vital market information which could quickly identify additional sales opportunities for operators.

> Iain Anderson is the General Manager of a large luxury hotel in Solihull, West Midlands. Similar to many of his competitors, he faced a forecasted reduction in overseas trade, but has undertaken a variety of highly successful marketing activities designed to maintain traditional customer base and boost other tourist trade.
> 'Positive targeted marketing and sales activity is of vital importance to the industry if we do not wish to suffer further reductions in trade. We must market and sell aggressively and be prepared to both gamble and be innovative.'

Agencies assist operators in a variety of ways; they become part of the operator's wider sales force, increasing customer awareness and improving access.

Having looked at marketing consortiums and agencies, we now must turn to other bodies who assist the sales and marketing function.

TOURIST BOARDS AND AGENCIES

Within the UK there exist regional tourist boards, backed by local tourist information offices, and headed up by the British Tourist Authority. The English Tourist Board is active in both national and international markets, and the majority of these activities are at the taxpayers' expense! Over the past decade the tourist boards have been increasingly active in the promotion and selling of the country, its regions, its areas and tourism and hospitality facilities. Many regional and area boards have created working partnerships with their hospitality operators – developing joint promotions and marketing initiatives that enhance the marketing and sales function.

Sadly, the contribution the tourist boards provide is often rather underrated. Services operated could include:

- Promotion of a particular area, town or region utilising brochures, videos, leaflets and advertising.
- Studies and reports on business generated and forecasts of possible future business.
- Guides for visitors and tourists.
- Accommodation booking.
- Representation at travel trade fairs and international tourist conventions.
- Provision of information to hospitality operators on future events planned within the area or region.
- Major targeted campaigns to attract visitors to a region, area or town.

Proactive tourist boards also assist in changing customer attitudes towards an area. Glasgow's highly successful campaign during the late 1980s coinciding with the city's Garden Festival saw a measurable change in customer perception of the city. 1990 saw the city assume the title of European City of Culture. Other cities, such as Dundee, Bradford and Edinburgh, are now following Glasgow's aggressive marketing initiatives. All these activities directly assist hospitality operators within a particular region or area.

SELF-HELP GROUPS – AREA HOSPITALITY ASSOCIATIONS

Hospitality operators often form local associations whose membership will include hotels, guest houses, restaurants, tourist-facility operators and representatives from the local tourist office. Meeting regularly, the operators will be able to share information and experience, plan joint promotional

Fig. 4.10
PROMOTIONAL MATERIAL FROM THE TOURIST BOARDS OF ENGLAND, SCOTLAND AND WALES

campaigns, and negotiate collectively with agencies for major events. In some respects, they act as mini-localised informal marketing consortiums, enabling increased effectiveness in joint sales and marketing activities. Larger associations may also involve themselves in shared advertising and promotional campaigns. They also are able, due to their position, to apply pressure to local authorities to improve tourist and visitor access.

While the competitive nature of the market creates certain problems for such associations, we may see a growth in such self-help groups as increasing numbers of operators recognise the benefits of proactive membership.

CONCLUSION

Hospitality operators recognising the increase in competition and the change in market demand seek additional direct or indirect channels of distribution. The contribution that booking organisations, marketing consortiums and other agencies can make to the improvement of business is easily recognised.

The growth in specialisation of such agencies supports the increasing segmentation of the hospitality market. While many of the agencies offer particular services to those offering accommodation or conference facilities, other operators gain indirectly from the sales and marketing activities they undertake.

The development of marketing strategy and sales and promotion activity should be planned in recognition of the services and benefits available from such agencies.

Marketing groups are often formed by individuals in specialist types of markets; an example of this is a group of hotels and bed and breakfast establishments.

> Distinctly Different is a marketing group made up of over 42 members in the UK who offer bed and breakfast accommodation in unusual properties, organised by Peter and Priscilla Roberts who operate their own bed and breakfast business from a converted windmill in Bradford upon Avon. The Roberts identified that their customers were interested in staying in other sympathetically converted premises.
>
> In the five years it has been operating, the group has developed informal, low-key but very effective marketing practices to promote such accommodation. Use has been made of regional tourist boards' various guides. The English Tourist Board has also assisted with the promotion of the properties overseas, especially to the American market.
>
> The Roberts run the marketing group as part hobby/part business and produce brochures and promotional leaflets for members.
>
> 'The running of the group while being very enjoyable has also assisted our own business.'

CHAPTER REVIEW

This chapter has concentrated on introducing the marketing and sales methods or actions most commonly utilised by operators following appropriate research and planning. As indicated, further activities are described in more detail in other chapters.

One important consideration is that the activities, methods and actions identified do not and should not operate in a vacuum. Effective marketing and sales attempts to integrate all actions into an overall strategy, increasing an operator's likelihood of success and positive return.

Additionally, such actions are not just aimed at outcomes, that is, increased business, but also concerned with creating awareness, understanding, developing further sales opportunities and providing ongoing analysis of generated business. Effective planning, control and evaluation is, then, of vital importance.

Within the section on advertising the need for appropriate targeting was identified, and this consideration holds true for all the actions outlined. The increased use of technology was identified to illustrate how much the increase in the speed of communication is affecting and assisting the industry.

Technology, whether it be the humble television or a central reservation system, increases the availability of products to the consumer through increasingly complex channels of product distribution. Such increased access to a company's products, facilities and services is also assisted by the various agencies and consortiums.

At this stage, you may wish to reread Chapter 2, which identified the primary factors operators consider prior to utilising some or all of the sales actions outlined in this chapter, prior to moving on to Chapter 5.

KEY POINTS

METHODS OF PLANNING AND CONTROL

- A variety of methods or actions exist which operators utilise.
- Marketing and sales is realistically concerned with actions and outcomes, not abstract concepts or theories.
- The identification of sales actions should be linked to considerations of the characteristics of the market and the organisation.
- Sales actions can be separated into indirect and direct activities, although the differentiation between the two is often difficult.
- Effective planning and control plays an increasingly important part of such activity.

ADVERTISING

- Advertising is designed to affect existing or potential customers' attitudes and buying behaviour.
- Advertising is only one part of the marketing and sales function and should be an outcome of appropriate research.
- Careful analysis should be undertaken on the results from advertising to identify the level of success.

SALES LITERATURE

- All operators utilise sales literature to some degree; whatever the type of material, the key elements are to ensure professional design and print, cost carefully, target effectively and evaluate regularly.

PUBLIC RELATIONS

- PR is an increasingly important element of marketing and sales activity, not only concerned with generating free publicity, but also improving the mutual understanding between the organisation and its public.

TELEPHONE SALES

- There exist three main uses of the telephone in respect of marketing and sales: research aimed at market research, proactive uses concentrating on developing sales opportunities and, lastly, reactive uses when personnel respond to sales enquiries.
- Telephone sales is a much used and abused sales method, which requires appropriate planning and particular skills.

USE OF TECHNOLOGY AND MEDIA

- The increasing complexity and competitiveness of the hospitality market will result in an increase in the use of technology in marketing and sales activity.

USE OF AGENCIES AND CONSORTIUMS

- Increasing numbers of operators will utilise a variety of agencies and consortiums to assist marketing and sales activities. Their use increases both customer awareness of their existence and channels of distribution.

QUESTIONS

- What factors should an operator consider when selecting a marketing and sales method or action?
- Describe the type of analysis an operator should undertake on the outcomes of a sales activity.
- Describe the common styles of advertising and explain the main advantages of each.
- List the guidelines for creating effective advertisements.
- Describe the sequence of planning in relation to the development of effective sales literature.
- If PR is the deliberate, planned and sustained effort to establish mutual understanding between an organisation and its public, explain the common types of activity which assist this process.
- Explain how effective telephone research can assist the operator in identifying additional sales opportunities and leads.
- Explain the advantages to independent operators in belonging to a marketing consortium.

CHAPTER FIVE

SALES SKILLS
AND TECHNIQUES

INTRODUCTION

This chapter will concentrate on some of the basic skills and knowledge required to sell hospitality products. There exist several texts available on what is described as the 'art of selling', referring to 'magic' elements of approach and method. While such techniques may have a certain relevance to some industries, positive selling within the hospitality industry should, I believe, be approached from a particular viewpoint.

No individual, be they a designated sales manager, a proprietor or a key member of staff, can sell effectively without an awareness and understanding of the products involved. Therefore, the first section outlines and stresses the importance for all staff involved in selling to possess sound product knowledge.

This understanding of the product range, availability and benefits should be matched to an understanding of how customers as individuals and groups react to sales activity. 'Consumer behaviour' outlines the factors which affect customer choice, and details some of the considerations sales staff will have when dealing directly with customers.

The process by which sales are achieved or lost is described within 'Stages of the selling process'. The understanding of how this basic process works and how, by its effective use, sales personnel can increase the likelihood of a positive outcome is explained.

With personal selling, there exist associated skills concerning how individuals react in a sales discussion. For the salesperson, it is important to both understand the barriers that can be created during a discussion, and how knowledge of personal selling skills can improve the likelihood of success. This aspect is dealt with in 'Face-to-face selling'.

Related to such personal skills is the aspect of how staff react with customers when, while not in a traditional direct selling situation, they are in fact still caring and selling. Without a doubt it is this aspect that has generated the largest amount of interest over the past few years. Operators are spending considerable amounts of money on staff training and systems to improve the standard and quality of care. The final section in this chapter deals with the importance of customer care, detailing how operators are increasingly accepting the contribution such activity has on maintaining and developing business.

The areas covered within this chapter are concerned with more personalised methods of selling. Such sales activity may be undertaken at the operator's unit or a client's workplace, and may be concerned with both generating initial business or maintaining and improving existing business. For many individuals within the industry, such activities create certain misgivings, and inexperienced newcomers to sales activity may often fear that some form of 'Arthur Daley' approach is required. Nothing is further from the truth. Experienced sales staff understand the importance of basing sales activities on caring for the customer and understanding that positive selling is concerned with creating professional relationships with prospective and existing customers.

CHAPTER LEARNING OBJECTIVES

By working through this chapter, completing the questions and some or all of the exercises in Appendix A, readers will be able to:

- Describe the importance of product knowledge in respect of assisting positive sales activity.
- Have an understanding of the role of all staff in the selling process.
- List the factors that affect customer buying behaviour, selection and choice.
- List the basic stages of the selling process and explain the key elements of each stage in respect of assisting positive outcomes.
- Have an understanding of the process of face-to-face selling and appreciate the need to reduce barriers to sales.
- Have an understanding of the importance of ongoing quality of customer care in relation to maintaining and developing business.

THE IMPORTANCE OF PRODUCT KNOWLEDGE

This section deals with the importance of knowledge of a company's products, goods, services and facilities by the staff and its relation to increasing initial sales, improving customer care and encouraging additional future sales. Lack of product knowledge by the staff can and does effect adversely overall sales volume. Staff in regular contact with customers should, therefore, have knowledge of all the company's goods, services and facilities.

Many hospitality companies and businesses now spend a considerable amount of time in ensuring that staff in regular contact with customers receive regular training in the importance of product knowledge, its relationship with customer care and increased sales, and basic skills of selling via an awareness of products.

UTILISING PRODUCT KNOWLEDGE

Personnel at all levels within hospitality units can utilise product knowledge and sales skills to positively affect sales volume. Product knowledge can be utilised to:

- Advise a potential client of the range of goods and services.
- Inform a client of the prices, costs and benefits of particular goods and services.
- Advise a customer of possible alternatives, that is, choices or options available.
- Direct customers to promotional items or event.
- Advise a customer of the difference in goods in terms of acceptability.
- Inform a customer of the actual make up of particular goods or items.
- Raise awareness of other services and facilities the company can offer.

Whether the individual concerned is the receptionist, bar person, food service assistant, sales manager or porter, he or she has a role to play in raising awareness of the range of goods, services and facilities, further assisting the possibility of an increase in sales.

However, for staff involved, knowledge of the range of products by itself is insufficient. Training should also provide individuals with the motivation, confidence and skills to sell positively. Without sound product knowledge, the staff cannot begin to assist in generating sales.

TRAINING

A minority of hospitality operators presume that staff will automatically be aware of the range of goods and services available, and be able to bring them to the attention of customers. They provide little or no training either at induction, or as an ongoing feature of individual or team training. The majority of hospitality operators employ a variety of training methods for all the staff. In research I carried out in 1992, of 28 companies canvassed, 85 per cent provided some form of product knowledge training.

TRAINING AT INDUCTION
Within the induction process, staff should receive instruction and information relating to:

- the company's overall product portfolio; and
- the specific products, services and facilities relevant to an individual's particular job or position.

After induction, training should be continued according to the type of business and the position staff hold.

PRODUCT SAMPLING TRAINING

This involves members of staff sampling the particular goods and services that they will be directly responsible for selling. While there are obvious cost considerations, such an activity allows the individual to sample at first hand products and services, thereby increasing their knowledge and confidence. An example of this would be when a new menu is planned, food production staff and food service staff can be involved in the testing and evaluation of dishes, both gaining from each other's expertise and both indirectly assisting future customers.

TEAM TRAINING

This method concentrates on the teams responsible for a particular area. Time will be spent on both reviewing the range of goods and services, and identifying additional sales ideas. The opportunity exists for staff in this review to discuss under-utilised services or low demand items to identify solutions to such sales problems.

BRIEFINGS

This could take the form of managers or supervisors briefing staff on particular promotions, products or services. The session may involve some of the methods already outlined, and is usually designed to assist the launch of a new or revised service or facility. Such briefings should include all affected staff as, in the end, they will be the ones receiving enquiries, dealing with purchases and assisting further sales. Training is often backed up by product information sheets, brochures or guides.

Whatever the type of training, the aim is to ensure that staff will have the necessary information to raise awareness of the product, increase sales and assist customer satisfaction.

FURTHERING THE PRODUCT KNOWLEDGE CONCEPT

Product knowledge is not just concerned with the physical aspects of a particular product, that is, the ingredients of a certain dish or cocktail. The concept includes other factors which are just as important, including:

- *The benefits associated with a particular product, service or facility,* for example: 'all our top-floor rooms have a lovely view'; or 'room 25 is a nice room'; or 'if you like to book a table in the restaurant before 7.30 pm, it is a little quieter then'.
- *Additional services and facilities a customer may not be aware of,* for example, leisure or conference facilities, opportunity for regular customers to join a discount scheme, or the ability to book directly other accommodation requirements.
- *On-selling of future events,* for example, a gourmet evening or quiz night.

CONFIDENCE BUILDING

Customers appreciate staff who can not only answer basic questions, such as 'What are the opening times?' or 'Can I get my dress cleaned?', but also appear to be both knowledgeable of, and interested in, other aspects of the unit's services. Such expressed knowledge creates increased confidence in the customer of the standard of care they will receive. Positive enquiries to customers and responses to queries create positive images, and positive images indirectly assist sales.

EXTERNAL PRODUCT KNOWLEDGE

While knowledge and understanding of a unit's product range is of vital importance in assisting customer care and sales, so too is knowledge of other services and facilities not directly related to the business. Information related to local and regional tourist and business facilities, local services and amenities can form an important addition to a unit's fund of customer information. This is obviously true in respect of operators dealing with accommodation. However, many hoteliers rely on the provision of leaflets displayed in the foyer, or a friendly receptionist to provide such information. Larger hotels may offer a concierge or enquiry service which concentrates on providing such information and assistance.

One enterprising independent hotelier provided his customers with road reports if he was aware of their particular route when leaving the establishment. While not directly selling his establishment, his system of obtaining 'knowledge' that affected his customers certainly aided indirectly future business.

SUMMARY

Busy operators often neglect the importance of providing new staff with appropriate knowledge of the product range, and many also fail to ensure ongoing updating of product knowledge information. Staff are important members of the operator's sales force, and should be provided with the knowledge of products, and the related skills to assist an increase in sales volume. However, increasing sales is only one aspect of this activity, and consideration must be given to the role product knowledge has in relation to customer care.

The following section identifies the importance of understanding how the customer will behave in relation to marketing and sales activities.

CONSUMER BEHAVIOUR

Operators need to have an understanding of the factors that affect customers in respect of their buying behaviour. Customers may be part of a recognisable group or market segment with certain common characteristics, but they are also individuals with their own particular needs and expectations. The way that individuals respond to sales messages will depend on a variety of complex psychological and physiological factors.

The identification of reasons why customers may or may not purchase is just as important as the identification of reasons why they may or do purchase. While an operator may not be able to solve all the reasons why customers do not purchase, identification of these reasons will aid the operator in minimising the factors.

THE FACTORS THAT AFFECT CUSTOMER BUYING BEHAVIOUR

Customers will purchase products, facilities and services for a variety of reasons.

NEED — THE BASIC FACTOR
There exists the element of basic need, for accommodation, food, drink, facilities, relaxation, information or enjoyment. The weary traveller, the hungry walker, the family on holiday or the culture-seeking tourist will all require services and facilities that satisfy these basic needs. The selection of the hospitality unit will be influenced by many other factors.

It is the operator's role to establish, via investigation, the level and location of such demand and, by utilisation of market research, identify the actual nature of the demand.

However, establishing that the population of an area is 250,000 and other statistical information is insufficient; the operator also needs to understand what encourages or dissuades customers from selecting their premises to satisfy basic needs.

INFLUENCES ON CUSTOMER BEHAVIOUR
Operators rely on marketing activities to identify general and specific customer needs. This may operate at the level of particular market segments, or at company or individual level by utilising telephone surveys, sales calls and presentations. Having identified potential demand and needs, the operator will require an understanding of what influences exist.

The main influences are as follows (but not necessarily in this order):

● *Location.* The ease of travel to and from a unit, its accessibility and availability. For a lodge hotel, this might mean siting close to motorway or major road routes; for a tourist hotel, it may mean location close to areas of natural beauty or other amenities.

- *Cost/value/quality*. The operators may run a highly priced facility or a low-cost one. Customers may require (and increasingly do nowadays) value in terms of goods, products and quality in return for their expenditure. They may be attracted to premises offering low prices or high prices, for example.
- *Sole supplier*. The unit may be the only supplier of the type of product required, or competition may be minimal.
- *Product and facility range*. The actual product range may be the one that best fits both the customer needs and expectations. The influence here is, perhaps, functionally based.
- *Style and ambience*. Customers will prefer different styles of operations; some may prefer very formalised levels of service, while others may be influenced by the provision of loud music and informality. Additionally, some customers will react negatively to premises that appear expensive.
- *Company purchased*. For many individuals, the selection of the facility is taken away from them. The company paying for facilities may have a fixed price range, or ongoing contracts with certain suppliers. Exhibition, function and conference organisers will have taken responsibility for booking facilities, leaving the individual with little or no choice in his or her selection.
- *Recommendation*. Customers are part of the indirect sales team, and their comments will influence to varying degrees other potential customers.
- *Advertising*. There is no doubt that effective advertising can influence customer buying behaviour. The famous coffee adverts in the early 1990s created huge additional demand for a particular brand. Advertising conducted by the hospitality industry seeks to create similar influence on the customer. While this aspect is discussed in Chapter 4, it is important to realise the degree of influence advertising exerts both positively and negatively.
- *Previous experience*. If the customer has enjoyed past experiences in respect of the unit, there will exist an in-built preference influence. Other operators may offer similar services and facilities; however, the customer will be used to, and is comfortable and familiar with, a particular one. Future buying behaviour will then be targeted on the preferred visit with an in-built resistance to change – a risk factor.
- *Environmental influences*. In some respects similar to location (above), environmental influences include the degree of acceptability of the unit in terms of its appearance.
- *Quality influences*. The actual or perceived quality of products, services and facilities will create a strong influence on consumers, especially if they have utilised the unit previously.

While all the listed factors provide direct influences on past or potential customers, each is an individual and the operator may also need to be aware of how other factors, such as age, gender, social background, and social status, will influence and affect the individual in respect of buying behaviour.

Summary

The influences that exist which affect buying behaviour are quite varied. While individuals and market segments may possess common basic needs, the reasons why they purchase are fairly complex. The operator will want to identify these influences and utilise knowledge of them in proactive and reactive marketing and sales activities.

The importance of recognising how individuals react to such activities, especially more personal sales activities, and how barriers can be created, influencing in a negative fashion potential business, is dealt with in the next two sections, 'Stages of the selling process' and 'Face-to-face selling'.

Stages of the selling process

Selling is a personal activity and process, differing from non-personal methods of selling, such as advertising. The term 'selling process' is most commonly used when describing the stages where a salesperson and potential clients meet face to face. The manner in which these stages are dealt with will affect not only the possibility of an immediate sale, but also future sales developed from such activity.

This section deals with the process and stages involved in the direct communication between salesperson and client, whether or not this is face to face. Taken in its most basic form, the process has three distinct stages:

- opening the sale;
- developing the sale; and
- closing the sale.

While the stages have obvious links, there exist particular considerations and priorities for each stage from both the viewpoint of the client and salesperson. Both parties have aims, needs and expectations. The client's aim may be quality service or reduction in price, while the salesperson's considerations may centre on the particular organisational needs. *The salesperson's main aim should be to effect a sale that satisfies the customer's requirements while ensuring profitable business for the organisation.*

When both parties are experienced in the process, the actual time spent may be minimal, with both parties quickly arriving at a compromise that is satisfactory. When one or both parties are inexperienced, the process may at best take longer or, at worst, result in either a bad sale or no sale at all. Whatever the situation, the experienced salesperson's role is to obtain the correct information, seek additional benefit and achieve a profitable sale.

The stages and their purpose

The main aims of each stage are as follows:

- *First stage – opening the sale.* The salesperson seeks to create empathy with the client and to identify precisely the client's requirements.
- *Second stage – developing the sale.* Having clearly established the basic requirements, the salesperson seeks to identify and satisfy other sales opportunities.
- *Third stage – closing the sale.* The salesperson moves to both obtain the sale, and confirm final details with an indication of the next action.

This process may take minutes, hours or even weeks. Whatever the time span, it is still important for the salesperson to keep to these basic steps, which provide a positive framework for a professional sales approach. Let us look at this process in more detail, identifying the characteristics of each stage and the possible barriers that may arise.

Stage one – opening the sale

There are several different situations related to this first stage.

New clients
In such a situation, the salesperson will need to provide background information related to their unit or company; additionally, the client may be already utilising other companies and will want to identify the benefits of changing 'supplier'. The salesperson then has the dual challenge of creating empathy with the client and selling the product in the face of competition.

If this meeting is being held within operator's premises, the salesperson has the advantage of being able to provide a sampling or viewing of the range of facilities and services. However, such 'tours' require an element of preparation which busy operators often fail to consider.

With new clients, the emphasis has to be on creating a favourable impression of the particular company, in addition to identifying initial requirements.

Negotiating with the wrong person
Individuals within companies given responsibility for making enquiries or arranging facilities may not have the final say when it comes to actual purchase decision. They may be seeking details of block bookings, one-off conference facilities, attempting to arrange a company promotional event or function. Experienced sales staff, especially within the hotel sector, will often be able to recognise when the individual lacks the appropriate authority and also recognise individuals who are 'time wasting'.

Simple questions directed at the individual at this first stage will usually ascertain the degree of authority an individual has, ensuring that time and effort is targeted correctly.

In situations when dealing with major business enquiries, the sales person may have to provide presentations to a variety of individuals in an effort to reach the decision maker.

COMMON PROBLEMS ASSOCIATED WITH THIS STAGE

Insufficient preparation by the salesperson. The salesperson has either not had the time or has prepared inadequately for the meeting. In certain circumstances, prior preparation may not be possible. However, when dealing with prospective clients on their own premises or conducting a pre-arranged meeting, the salesperson should obtain sufficient appropriate information about the client.

Lack of product knowledge and negotiating authority. The importance of product knowledge was described above. The salesperson should not only possess all the required information, but also be in a position to actually negotiate the sale. If the salesperson has to defer pricing decisions to a more senior person, the question must be asked, why were they negotiating in the first place?

Failure to create the correct relationship with the client. Experienced sales staff will possess the appropriate interpersonal and communication skills to ensure a positive start to negotiation. Inexperienced staff may create both personal and physiological barriers to establishing an appropriate rapport between seller and client. Meetings conducted in a noisy area with interruptions or from behind a desk will hardly induce confidence in the client.

Failure to obtain the appropriate information. At this first stage the salesperson is seeking to identify information related not only to the customer's requirements, but also necessary background information concerning the customer. The initial information provides the basis on which the salesperson can possibly develop the sale, obtaining additional benefit to both the customer and the organisation.

STAGE TWO – DEVELOPING THE SALE

In certain circumstances, there exists the opportunity for the salesperson to develop the sale further, by exploring additional mutual benfits. The salesperson will seek to discuss the potential business in more detail, obtaining information about possible additional needs. For example, an enquiry for basic accommodation may result in the identification of requirements for meeting facilities, provision of upgraded rooms, a special menu, travel assistance and associated public relations activity.

COMMON PROBLEMS ASSOCIATED WITH THIS STAGE

Attempting to sell too much. Having identified the customer's basic requirements, the salesperson then proceeds to attempt to sell everything else, providing details of all the company's or unit's facilities and services. They are then moving far away from the customer's real requirements and needs.

Rushing the process. Having possibly obtained the business, the salesperson rushes through this stage, missing the opportunity to identify additional sales and, more importantly, neglecting to obtain clearly all the necessary information.

STAGE THREE — CLOSING THE SALE

This stage is concerned with both obtaining the business, if appropriate, and ensuring all details are correct. Both parties require a positive outcome and a clear understanding of this stage.

A typical conversation could be 'Well, Mr Roberts, I would like to make the reservation for you; it's for . . . and includes . . .' The salesperson is then moving to receive verbal confirmation that the sale will go through and identify again the components of the agreement.

COMMON PROBLEMS ASSOCIATED WITH THIS STAGE

Failure to confirm details. For basic accommodation reservations, the information required is fairly straight forward. However, for functions, block bookings, weddings or conference business the information is more complex. Naturally, such agreements will be completed in a written form, but failure to confirm details of requirements correctly at this stage (on both sides) will lead to delay, possible confusion and even the cancellation of the business.

Allowing the client to take control. In a service industry where identifying and satisfying customer needs is seen as the key to marketing and sales, to suggest that there is a problem in allowing the customer to take control appears to be contradictory. However, there exists the risk of attempting to over-satisfy requirements that may not be satisfied, or providing too many benefits to the customer, resulting in possible reduction of revenue and profits.

FACE-TO-FACE SELLING

This type of selling is commonplace within the hospitality industry, and is often utilised when potential clients visit the hotel, restaurant or facility. This will often be the first visit the client has made to the establishment, and the salesperson has the ideal situation to effect a positive sale.

Face-to-face selling is a difficult skill to master and individuals with years of experience still make mistakes. Over-confidence can be just as damaging as lack of preparation. The key considerations in this process are:

- Preparation by the salesperson; obtaining information about the client before his or her arrival, and information related to his or her request.
- Ensuring the client is welcomed and appropriate staff are informed about the appointment.
- Attempting to create empathy by introducing him or herself, and being friendly rather than familiar.
- Using an appropriate place for discussion with no physical or mental barriers being created, for example, an overloaded desk, a constantly ringing telephone, and the client in a lower chair than the salesperson.
- Listening to the client carefully.
- Clarifying with the client his or her requirements.
- Conducting a showround – having first ensured that all facilities are set up appropriately.
- Finalising with the client the agreement and explaining the next action to be taken.

However, there are pitfalls to this process which will, if not recognised, cause a loss of not only one particular sale, but potentially many more. The successful salesperson will have:

- sound product knowledge;
- good listening skills;
- authority to negotiate terms;
- knowledge of the effects of poor body language;
- experience in the process of the sale, that is, opening, developing and closing a sale; and lastly

- an enthusiasm and commitment to the product, service or facility he or she is selling.

For the establishment the salesperson is the ambassador and the client will want assurance that his or her requirements will be met. Wherever the meeting takes place, the hospitality salesperson will want to effect a sale.

> Sally Elsdon is Conference and Banqueting Sales Manager for the Four Seasons Inn-on-the-Park Hotel, London: 'Preparation is of vital importance, you must complete research on the client or company and potential business. The sales presentation should be limited when appropriate to ten minutes, geared towards the client and their particular needs and budgets. It is important to listen to the client and establish empathy. Every client is special and so are their planned events. Following the sales presentation, a follow-up letter should be sent, thanking the client and confirming the next action. Successful selling is concerned with continuity of care.'

Many operators will conduct sales presentations in a similar way. Having obtained prior information about the company or individual, their task is then to both create the right impression and obtain appropriate information.

The limit of ten minutes which Sally Elsdon quotes can create the appropriate image: 'allow me ten minutes of your time to explain the additional benefits my organisation can offer'. However, there exist situations where strict time limits are inappropriate. Certain clients may prefer more formal presentations, especially if the contract is large or of considerable cost. Additionally, certain nationalities may have a particular style of completing business.

One overseas market that has attracted considerable attention over the past few years is the Japanese. With the increase in the number of Japanese companies within the UK and a growth up until the early 1990s of Japanese tourists, many hospitality operators have targeted this market to great effect. A clear understanding of the manner in which certain nationalities prefer to receive such sales presentations is required.

The American market will prefer in general an aggressive approach. In such situations, the salesperson requires not only knowledge of the company, but also an awareness and sensitivity in respect of cultural differences.

SALES AIDS USED IN PRESENTATIONS

The salesperson can utilise a variety of visual aids and sales material to reinforce the verbal presentation. This could include:

- Slides and videos: utilised for sales presentations to larger groups, either at company level or at travel and tourist exhibitions.

- Brochures and leaflets: these are usually best left with a prospective client to reinforce initial sales messages.
- Presentation pack: some salespersons may utilise a presentation portfolio, encompassing pictures and images of facilities and products. The salesperson may talk through such material in an attempt to illustrate the range and quality of provision. One hotel owner I know used such a pack to show particular layouts and photographs of dishes and buffets to potential clients for the unit's function room. However, such packs should be used only when customer needs have been clearly identified; utilisation prior to this prevents the salesperson from obtaining the correct information.

Whatever material is utilised, its role is to reinforce the information collected and provided by the salesperson, and it is not a replacement for effective personal sales presentation skills.

SUMMARY

Whether the sales situation is one conducted at the operator's premises or at the potential client's premises, there exist certain basic guidelines to creating appropriate sales. Appropriate preparation prior to the meeting provides the salesperson with a sound base on which to build a sale. Knowledge both of the product, and the factors that will affect a potential client's response to such a situation, assists both parties in working towards a mutually satisfying agreement. The overall emphasis should be on care, related both to the manner in which sales meetings are conducted and to the customer.

The final section in this chapter will look in more detail at this aspect, and the importance of customer care to hospitality operators.

THE IMPORTANCE OF CUSTOMER CARE

If identifying customer needs is the first element in the marketing and sales process, positive customer care can be identified as the last element, completing the cycle of activities aimed at maintaining and developing profitable business.

While the importance of customer care has been noted elsewhere in this book, it is worth repeating the old premise that 'satisfied customers usually return'. Marketing and sales activities are not just aimed at identifying customer needs, but satisfying these needs. The satisfaction of customers may originate from benefits including value for money, quality, level and range of facilities, products and services.

This section will concentrate on customer care, exploring the basic methods and identifying the contribution it makes to appropriate business development.

THE BACKGROUND TO CUSTOMER CARE

While it can be recognised that positive customer care is a current trend within the industry, it is in reality nothing new. In their day, hospitality operators such as Gordons Hotels, British Transport Hotels and Butlins all practised versions of this approach within their establishments. In the great Victorian hotel era, the customer was fêted and cosseted in many cases to a higher degree than exists today. What has altered is the degree of general awareness of the need to improve standards and quality, concentrating activities on ensuring a more positive approach to an element that was perhaps characterised by elements of servility.

THE CASE FOR POSITIVE CUSTOMER CARE

Within the previous section on consumer behaviour, the importance of understanding the psychological factors which affect customers was explained. Having entered a hospitality premises the operator should continue to consider the various effects the provision of service, goods and facilities will have.

While accepting this premise, the case for positive customer care rests on practical considerations, including:

- The provision of a quality product or service.
- The provision of products, services and facilities that represent value for money.
- The need to ensure customers receive what they paid for and what the operator has been contracted to provide.
- The requirement to minimise complaints.
- The requirement to be able to respond to any complaints positively, reducing the possibility of additional lost sales.
- The realisation that, by ensuring all of the above, satisfied customers usually return and become additional members of the operator's sales team.
- The realisation that, due to the increasingly competitive nature of the business, the growing sophistication of the market and the alteration in the customer's general expectations, if an operation *does not* seek to establish sound customer care practices, it will lose business to other operators.

Customer care is sound business strategy and practice.

THE BASIC ELEMENTS OF CUSTOMER CARE

Customer care is concerned with:

- The provision of quality products, facilities and services.

Fig. 5.1
IN PROMOTING CUSTOMER CARE, ATTENTION
TO DETAIL ENSURES SUCCESS

- The expression of care for the customer regardless of whether they are regular customers, new customers, high or low spenders: 'I expect my staff to treat all customers as important, and provide the same level of care and attention whether they utilise our premises once a year or once a week' – a hotel and restaurant proprietor.
- Ensuring the possibility of dissatisfaction with services is minimised and if they occur staff react appropriately: 'While we strive to minimise complaints, we provide staff with training of how to react to complaints' – a restaurant manager.

Customer care practices commence prior to guests entering the unit, with the provision of staff training. Such training could include:

- product knowledge and skills;
- complaint handling;
- attitudinal training.

This could be expressed as the three Cs of customer care: commitment, customer, care. The customers in their relation to premises go through a process or cycle of events, all of which must be analysed to identify potential problems.

Customer care related to enquiries

Whether a customer makes a written, personal or telephone enquiry, there exists the potential for problems related to special and efficient response and sales opportunities. Therefore, staff handling enquiries should be trained to respond correctly, obtain or 'translate' the information required and follow up effectively.

Customer care related to arrivals

Whether the customer is arriving to utilise accommodation, facilities or partake of food and beverages, there need to be appropriate processes for ensuring the customer is received correctly.

Many of the larger hotels have altered their traditional reception desks to a more personalised, informal style. For regular customers or individuals attending overnight conferences, an 'express check in' service may be provided.

Staff within other hospitality establishments are also trained to ensure the appropriate reception of customers. Different styles of approach obviously exist. Fast-food operators may train staff to offer a brief but friendly greeting, while certain types of themed restaurants will train the food service person to not only greet the customer, but also introduce themselves and provide initial descriptions of services available.

Whatever the technique, the emphasis is on the customer being received appropriately and efficiently, attempting to create at the outset positive relationships and care for the customer.

Customer care related to unit utilisation

While the customer is on the premises and utilising facilities and services, the operator aims to ensure the experience is a positive one. The efficiency of service, the quality of products, the provision of facilities and, most importantly, the relationship with the customer all affect the quality of the customer experience.

While problems may occur from the operator's side, it must also be accepted that not all customers will respond positively themselves. They may be tired, anxious, nervous, unsure and, as experienced hospitality staff will know, just plain awkward. Positive customer care training will involve staff in having both an understanding of the factors that may affect a customer's response, and how to deal with the few but genuinely awkward customers.

CUSTOMER CARE RELATED TO DEPARTURES AND FEEDBACK

The departure of customers from a premises, either hotel or restaurant and the feedback they may provide, is the last element in the cycle of care. The handling of bills, luggage, transfer on to other units and the receipt of feedback all require appropriate handling. While there may exist certain formalities or systems to go through, for example, checking out of a hotel, or leaving a restaurant, there exists a considerable amount that operators can do to reduce customer dissatisfaction. Systems can be made more efficient and personal, with the emphasis on providing the departing customer with a final but, hopefully, lasting and positive memory.

In my research on this subject, I discovered hoteliers who provided a windscreen clean service, produced road reports on any travel problems, provided jump leads for drivers who had car battery problems, and efficient luggage handling. The manner and style of language is also important with staff training directed at ensuring positive and friendly additional sales messages.

Often on departure an enquiry may be made to ascertain the customer's degree of satisfaction. While this is important if this is the first opportunity the customer has had to comment on the quality of provision, responses will not be particularly helpful to the operator.

It is with this final aspect where the emphasis should be, customers being involved in the process right from the start of the 'contract' and provided with appropriate opportunities for commenting on the provision and bringing to the attention of staff any inadequacies. To have customers leave dissatisfied and then complain later when the damage has been done, or worse not return, is the situation customer care practices seek to avoid.

Positive customer care does increase spend per head. On a recent visit to Nottingham, I entered the Bella Pasta restaurant. The management and staff had obviously considered the importance of care skills. I was greeted quickly, escorted to a table, assisted with seating and quickly brought a menu and asked politely if I required a drink.

All this should be standard throughout the industry, each customer being treated as important and provided with pleasant service. The attitude towards customers should be positive and in this restaurant they certainly practised this aspect well.

When the meal was brought to the table I was asked: 'Would you like some additional cheese?' and 'I hope you enjoy your meal.' During the meal a check was made to see that everything was satisfactory. The bill was brought to the table efficiently, again a check was made: 'Is everything satisfactory?' Upon leaving I was thanked for my custom and handed a comment card and the restaurant business card. The last message was: 'Please call again.'

In this restaurant, the staff exhibited real care for the customer alongside practical and effective selling skills. Within the restaurant, additional merchandising displays and posters raised awareness of 'offers'. Finally, there were various leaflets for customers to take away (an example of which is

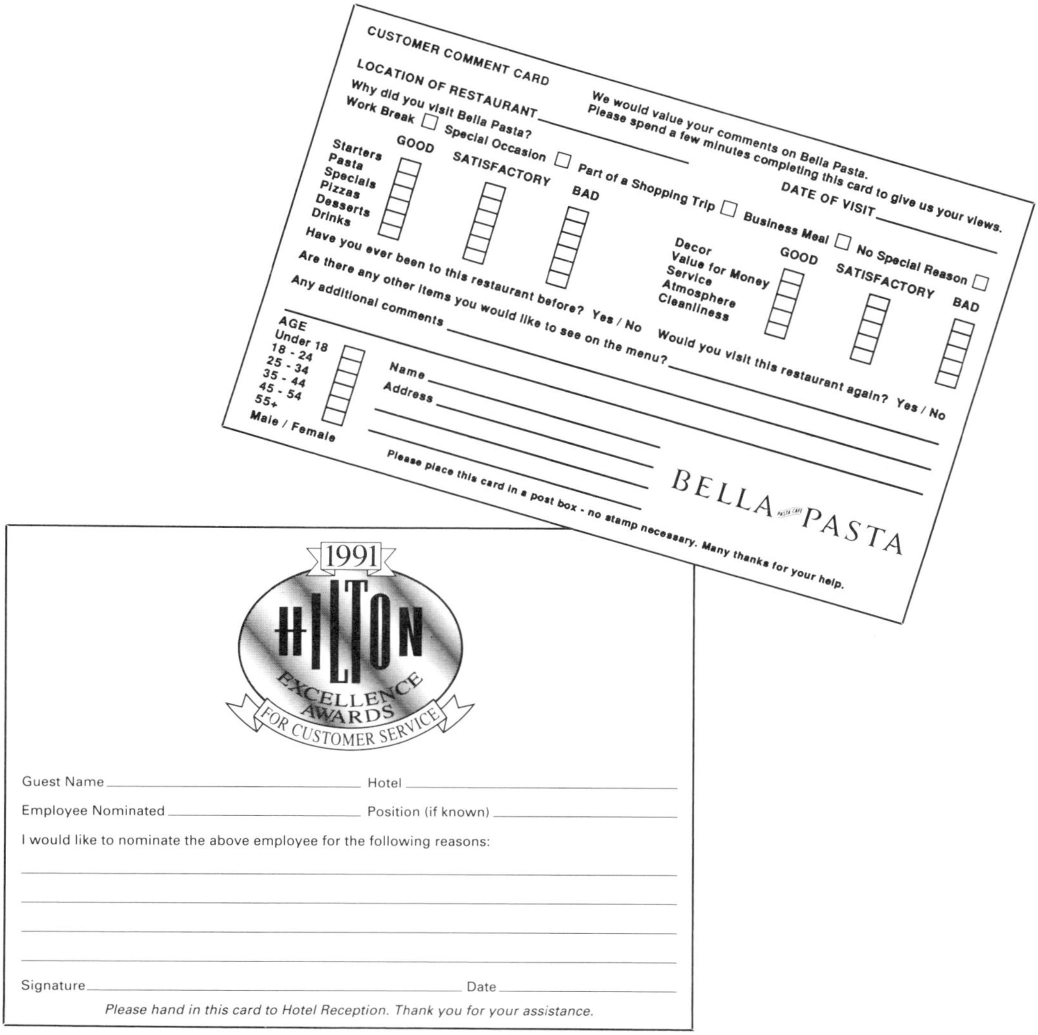

CUSTOMER COMMENT CARD

LOCATION OF RESTAURANT ____ We would value your comments on Bella Pasta. Please spend a few minutes completing this card to give us your views.

DATE OF VISIT ____

Why did you visit Bella Pasta?

Work Break ☐ Special Occasion ☐ Part of a Shopping Trip ☐ Business Meal ☐ No Special Reason ☐

	GOOD	SATISFACTORY	BAD
Starters	☐	☐	☐
Pasta	☐	☐	☐
Specials	☐	☐	☐
Pizzas	☐	☐	☐
Desserts	☐	☐	☐
Drinks	☐	☐	☐

	GOOD	SATISFACTORY	BAD
Decor	☐	☐	☐
Value for Money	☐	☐	☐
Service	☐	☐	☐
Atmosphere	☐	☐	☐
Cleanliness	☐	☐	☐

Have you ever been to this restaurant before? Yes / No Would you visit this restaurant again? Yes / No

Are there any other items you would like to see on the menu? ____

Any additional comments ____

AGE
Under 18 ☐
18 - 24 ☐
25 - 34 ☐
35 - 44 ☐
45 - 54 ☐
55+ ☐
Male / Female

Name ____

Address ____

BELLA PASTA

Please place this card in a post box - no stamp necessary. Many thanks for your help.

1991 HILTON EXCELLENCE AWARDS FOR CUSTOMER SERVICE

Guest Name ____ Hotel ____

Employee Nominated ____ Position (if known) ____

I would like to nominate the above employee for the following reasons:

Signature ____ Date ____

Please hand in this card to Hotel Reception. Thank you for your assistance.

Fig. 5.2

HOTEL AND RESTAURANTS MAY PRINT CUSTOMER COMMENT CARDS TO INCREASE CUSTOMER FEEDBACK. A CUSTOMER IS ASKED, ON LEAVING, TO COMMENT ON VALUE FOR MONEY, FOOD QUALITY, HYGIENE AND OTHER CUSTOMER CARE ISSUES

included below). This operation was utilising a variety of positive yet simple customer care and selling techniques to great effect.

Such activities are often seen as only affecting captive customers. Yet what was the effect of the operator's sales techniques? That afternoon I attended two meetings and additionally spoke to several people. To the majority I mentioned the good meal and service I received, and I have included it in this text. Not perhaps an example of large-scale selling, but a good example of getting customers to sell an establishment by recommendation.

Summary

Positive customer care techniques are the last element of the sales cycle. The experience the customer enjoys is the outcome of all the other marketing and sales activity. If the experience is a negative one, then additional market research, advertising, sales actions and promotional activities may fail to recapture the lost customer. Additionally, as a member of the unit's sales team, the customer begins to affect other potential sales.

The final chapter in this text will look at how activities related to increasing sales volume can assist both profit and ongoing marketing and sales actions.

Chapter review

This chapter has concentrated on what many see as the sharp end of marketing and sales activity, that is, personal sales actions. The elements of product knowledge, consumer behaviour, selling processes and customer care make up what I would refer to as a 'personal selling overview'. Each is dependent on the others, a process which is circular starting and ending with the customer.

Having identified needs, understood and negotiated possible sales barriers and successfully sold products, the whole relationship can be permanently damaged by inadequate customer care.

Selling is, perhaps, an art, but not a pure one. There exists a science of methodology, practices and approaches that sales staff can undertake to improve sales and revenue.

The activity related to increasing sales volume is dealt with in Chapter 6.

Key points

- There exists a variety of skills related to the process identified as selling.
- Selling hospitality products, services and facilities should be related to identifying and satisfying customer needs profitably.
- For an individual to sell effectively, he or she requires knowledge of the products he or she is involved in.
- Customers will have a variety of reasons for purchasing and a series of factors will affect their purchasing behaviour. Sales staff should have an understanding of what factors will affect a customer in relation to purchasing behaviour.
- The majority of sales can be broken down into a three-stage approach of opening, developing and closing a sale. While a simplified analysis, an

understanding of the elements of each stage and a knowledge of possible
barriers to sales will increase a salesperson's ability to obtain and develop
profitable business.

- In face-to-face sales situations, the salesperson needs to be aware of the
psychological and physiological aspects that affect sales.
- Careful consideration should be given to increasing the standard of
customer care and recognition made of its contribution to developing and
maintaining business.

QUESTIONS

- List the type of selling skills required by a hotel receptionist.
- Explain the importance of sound product knowledge for *all* staff within a
hospitality unit, and outline methods by which staff can be trained 'to have
knowledge'.
- List the external factors that may affect customer choice or buying
behaviour.
- Explain the importance of understanding the reasons why customers
purchase products, facilities or services.
- What preparation should a salesperson make prior to: conducting a sales
meeting at the client's premises; and conducting a sales meeting at the
hospitality unit.
- Explain the contribution positive customer care practices make to indirect
sales and promotional activity.

CHAPTER SIX

THE CONCEPT AND PRACTICE OF IN-HOUSE SELLING

INTRODUCTION

This chapter is concerned with activities relating to improving sales once the customer has entered the premises. It will cover the following areas:

- the importance of positive in-house selling;
- an outline of basic methods;
- its relation to the various sections of the industry;
- staff and team training and motivation;
- in-house campaigns and promotions; and
- merchandising

Reference will be made to other related topics, such as personal selling skills, product knowledge and consumer behaviour, which are discussed in Chapter 5.

> **A DEFINITION OF IN-HOUSE SELLING**
> A useful basic definition would be: selling activities concerned with increasing average customer spend.

Hospitality operators spend considerable amounts of revenue on a variety of techniques in an attempt to attract customers to their premises. However, attracting customers into a premises is just the start of the complete sales process. Once on the premises, the customer, whether purchasing accommodation, facilities or food and beverages, presents other sales opportunities. The hospitality operator will seek to maximise on these opportunities, undertaking activities that will encourage further sales. Such activities could include basic product promotion, merchandising at the point of sale, in-house advertising and person-to-person selling techniques.

However successful, in-house selling involves more complex considerations which relate to the complete way in which the unit operates, including the presentation of sales information to the captive customer, the training and attitude of staff and the manner in which customers react to possible increased sales pressure. Selling is said to be a personal activity involving the customer and seller in forms of verbal communication. Yet to exclude some forms of non-personal selling, such as merchandising, would be to ignore the influence such activities have on the person approach. It is useful, then, to look briefly at why such activities are so important to both the operator and the customer.

In the past, hospitality operators were seemingly reluctant to undertake in-house selling activities – the activities appeared to stop once the customer had entered the premises. There existed a variety of reasons for this approach, including the type of market, the relative unsophistication of general demand, lack of competition and a lack of understanding among the industry of the positive aspects of proactive selling and promotion.

Customer care techniques may have been practised, but they were not recognised as part of the selling process rather directed towards an element of servility. During the mid-1970s there emerged operators who capitalised on a more aggressive sales approach within their establishments. The Bistingo chain of bistros/restaurants, popular in London during this period, utilised fairly basic techniques, such as menus on windows and promotions, to increase customer spend very effectively. The famous Hard Rock Café situated on the corner of Park Lane in London still packs customers in. In its early days, it utilised a range of techniques that encouraged increased spend. The establishment has now created a mini-merchandising and promotion industry of its own, with Hard Rock memorabilia and clothing items being widely sought.

However successful, this style of approach is inappropriate for some organisations. However, a considerable number of operators do provide items with the company or unit's logo on. Merchandised items are only one element of in-house selling, and their use is to back up other activities that concentrate on the customer.

Any positive activity that can increase in-house sales and contribute to effective customer care is worth considering. The sections that follow will describe the importance of such practices and provide details of their utilisation within various sectors of the industry.

THE IMPORTANCE OF IN-HOUSE SELLING

The operator seeks to satisfy customers while making a profit. The amount of profit is affected by a variety of factors, such as costs, revenue and sales volume. By increasing sales volume, that is, the number of customers multiplied by the average spend per head, the operator can increase the return, profit or yield on goods and services, presuming that there exists positive control on revenue and costs. However positive in-house selling is, it should not just be concerned with increasing sales, but linked closely to customer care practices.

The importance of this aspect is being increasingly accepted in the UK hospitality industry. In a survey I conducted over 70 establishments during 1991, over 85 per cent identified the provision of customer care training for personnel related to improving sales as their priority for the following year.

The hospitality industry in the late 1980s and early 1990s faced both increased competition and reduction in demand. When such a situation exists it is even more important to encourage and assist an increase in sales from proactive in-house sales and promotion activities.

THE CONTRIBUTION OF IN-HOUSE SALES AND PROMOTION ACTIVITIES

Earlier in this chapter I identified that such activity should not just be aimed at increasing customer spend – although this is obviously an important element. The contribution effective in-house sales and promotion activities makes can be detailed as follows:

INCREASED PROFIT OR YIELD

In periods of recession, reduction or alteration in demand, the operator will often be pressurised to reduce costs. The potential amount of revenue available from individual customers or groups, therefore, needs to be increased wherever possible. While some activities may only generate small amounts of additional revenue per head, such amounts when totalled with other activities can substantially alter an organisation's or unit's overall performance.

We can utilise the example of additional liquor sales in a restaurant to illustrate this aspect. If the average number of customers in a restaurant is 45 per evening and existing average spend per head is £22, the average take equals £990 per evening. Staffing training is provided concentrating on increasing pre-dinner drinks, with dinner wine and speciality coffees or liqueur sales. Assuming that the restaurant personnel utilises both product knowledge and customer care skills effectively and increase revenue by 20 per cent, that is, £198, they have generated nine extra customers without external advertising or promotion.

Twenty per cent would appear quite a high increase, and in certain circumstances may not be achievable. However, many operators do little to promote increase spend in their restaurants, and even a 5 per cent increase would in effect provide the equivalent of just over two customers. If this was repeated every night, the total annual additional income would be (at 20 per cent) £11,880, or 540 equivalent customers.

Increased profits can be generated from other areas, and all operators have specific opportunities to increase profit or yield by effective in-house methods.

IMPROVED CUSTOMER CARE AND SATISFACTION

In general, customers appreciate and respond to caring and knowledgeable staff. While they may reject a hard sell approach, they generally appreciate activities designed to enhance their experience. Surveys conducted on customers' priority in terms of service over the past few years have highlighted the importance of 'friendly service', 'knowledgeable staff' and 'quality of attitude' against factors such as speed of service, cost or quality of food.

This aspect of quality is becoming increasingly important, and many operators within the industry are utilising British Standard 5750 to adapt their working practices, especially in terms of customer care, to improve standards.

Many elements of effective in-house selling and promotions contribute to positive customer care, and when customers are satisfied or happy with their experience, they generally increase spending and, more importantly, return to the unit.

MOTIVATION OF STAFF

Staff perform a vital function in respect of in-house sales and promotion. without appropriate training they will possibly lack the necessary skills to postively affect sales. With incorrect attitudes they may *adversely* affect sales. For all its pressures, work within the industry is a team activity. Individuals may possess varying degrees of skills or knowledge. Lack of skills among certain staff may be overcome with a positive team approach to sales and promotion. (The aspect of training and motivation is dealt with later in this chapter.) By involving all staff with in-house sales and promotion, the operator provides a focus for effort, commitment, and individual and team satisfaction.

Where staff identify increased sales and customer satisfaction directly through their efforts, their own satisfaction and commitment will be increased, which in turn affects other customers. Staff become 'co-owners' of the organisation, and this assists not only their general motivation, but also assists further in-house selling and promotion.

OPPORTUNITIES FOR SALES SPONSORSHIPS AND PARTNERSHIPS

Within certain limitations, in-house sales and promotions also provide opportunities for the operator to link with other companies, operators, agencies and organisations. Very effective promotions can be generated in partnership with other bodies, which contribute to the operator's ability to attract and satisfy a wider market.

At a low level, this may be a special evening for 'brides to be', where the operator links with businesses offering related services. At a higher level, operators may link with regional and national organisations offering specialist tourist facilities. The scope of the in-house promotion then increases and starts to create additional demand.

The opportunity to attract appropriate promotional partners may also provide additional contributions to the cost of particular promotions. Sponsorship then not only can widen the services available and increase access from specialist markets, but also assist with activity related costs.

CUSTOMER INVOLVEMENT

Customers are the life blood of any business. Their stay or utilisation of the operator's facilities may be only short lived. However, they can contribute to the additional promotion of a particular unit or company. Customers are in reality an important part of a business's sales team – although they may not often be aware of this fact!

The degree to which operators can involve customers in sales and promotional activity depends on the style of the establishment and the type of sales activity. The customers' contribution often occurs after and outside the event – 'we had a great time at the . . . the other night', or 'I recommend that place'. In a more lighthearted way, customers can also contribute to the success of certain types of in-house promotions and events, a factor long recognised by many publicans who offer quiz nights and karaoke evenings. Such activities which involve the customer are aimed both at providing increased customer satisfaction or enjoyment, and increasing average customer spend. For many establishments, quiz nights may be inappropriate. However, all will have visitors or guests who possess the ability to affect other potential customers (hopefully positively).

CAPTURE OF MARKETING INFORMATION

For many operators, the identification of visitors' or guests' names is difficult. While hotels and restaurants can utilise reservation or booking information to identify past customers, they may only 'capture' a percentage of such information. In-house sales and promotional activity can sometimes assist the operator by including a mechanism for capturing data within the activity. For instance, during the period of writing this book I left my business card in several Little Chefs, a Granada Lodge, two tourist facilities, two hotels and a restaurant. All were left in response to some form of competition or promotion. Such activities are fairly standard within certain sectors of the industry, although I might add I personally have not 'won' anything yet!

There exist other more subtle ways in which operators can capture marketing information, including guest comment cards and information request slips distributed to guests at dinners, functions and conferences. In addition, involving customers in promotional activities, the operator can identify potential 'targets' for other sales promotions or campaigns. Such contributions, although often on a relatively small scale, provide welcome assistance to an operator seeking to develop other businesses.

IMPROVEMENT IN STANDARDS

I have already identified the contribution that elements of in-house sales and promotional activities make to the business in regard to customer satisfaction and involvement and staff motivation. It must also be recognised that when such sales activities are effectively undertaken and are part of a professional regard for the customer, overall standards will improve.

Obviously, there exist many other factors that will affect standards, the contribution effective sales actions provide is to reinforce aspects of positive customer care.

Staff provided with the appropriate training become more confident in their particular tasks and in dealing with customers. This increased confidence can also assist staff when dealing with awkward customers and complaints.

As efforts and energies are directed at planning and operating effective in-house sales campaigns, the operator will become increasingly aware of any deficiencies in standards, and be likely to improve them. The constant and appropriate raising of standards contributes by providing customers with improved benefits.

SUMMARY

While all of these contributions will in the end increase customer spend, they also act to improve the general business performance. Such contributions should not be ignored.

Having identified the ways in which effective in-house sales and promotions can contribute it is now important to look in more detail at typical activities.

BASIC METHODS, PLANNING AND CONTROL

IN-HOUSE SELLING METHODS

There exist a variety of methods and activities the hospitality operator can utilise to increase total sales volume. The selection of these is dependent upon:

- the style and type of operation;
- the budget available;
- the skills and knowledge of staff involved;
- the type of product, service or facility the activity is aimed at.

EFFECTIVE PLANNING — THE FIRST CONSIDERATION

As with all marketing and sales activities, a positive in-house sales campaign requires careful planning. Such planning may be for larger organisations with branded outlets all selling similar products, a head office responsibility. With smaller organisations, the responsibility will lie directly with the management. Whatever the situation, careful and effective planning will assist the potential success of in-house sales activities.

Effective planning will identify all the necessary stages required and take into consideration the factors both internal and external that will affect possible success.

An example of the stages is provided in Figure 6.1.

The complexity of the planning is dependent on the scale of any particular campaign – and it would be too formal a structure in many situations, for example, a small hotel wishing to promote the take up of liqueurs.

Whatever the scale of the activity, appropriate effective planning is important. The prime considerations should be:

- Identification of the problem or opportunity.
- Identification of the aims, that is, what does the operator wish to do, increase sales of rooms, newspapers, liquor sales in restaurant, capture guest data, etc?
- Selection and planning of actions or methods.

Once these considerations have been satisfied, the operator has set the framework for sales and promotional activity. The aspect of planning and control will be returned to shortly.

BASIC IN-HOUSE SELLING AND PROMOTIONAL APPROACHES

Selling is often identified as a personal activity or transaction, that is, one that takes place between individuals. While many of the methods and approaches listed below do not fall easily into this category, undertaken effectively they all affect sales to varying degrees.

EFFECTIVE PLANNING STAGE

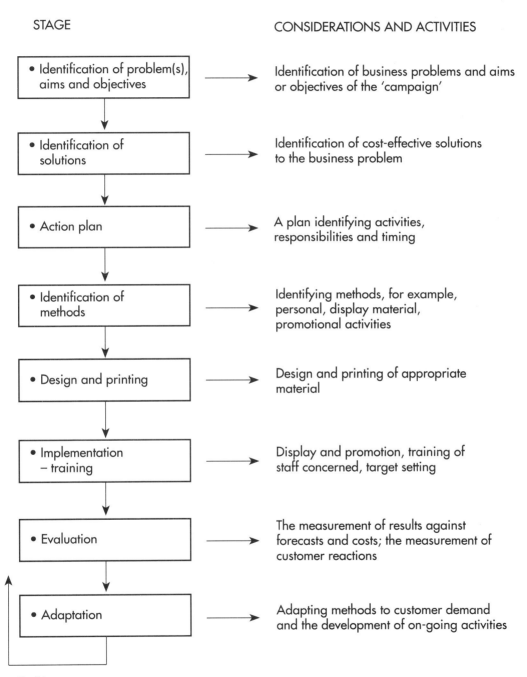

STAGE

CONSIDERATIONS AND ACTIVITIES

- Identification of problem(s), aims and objectives → Identification of business problems and aims or objectives of the 'campaign'

- Identification of solutions → Identification of cost-effective solutions to the business problem

- Action plan → A plan identifying activities, responsibilities and timing

- Identification of methods → Identifying methods, for example, personal, display material, promotional activities

- Design and printing → Design and printing of appropriate material

- Implementation – training → Display and promotion, training of staff concerned, target setting

- Evaluation → The measurement of results against forecasts and costs; the measurement of customer reactions

- Adaptation → Adapting methods to customer demand and the development of on-going activities

Fig. 6.1
EFFECTIVE PLANNING STAGES

DIRECT SALES ACTIVITIES

The operator here is concerned with encouraging additional sales of products and increased use of facilities. The captive customer is on the premises and may be using overnight accommodation, in a restaurant for a meal, or using a facility. They have already purchased a basic item and presumably satisfied their first need, that is, a room, food, drink or the opportunity to relax. Direct purchase activities are aimed at increasing average spend per head, and operators use a variety of techniques and approaches to encourage such increased spending.

DIRECT PROMOTIONAL ACTIVITIES

Here, the operator is concerned with promoting a particular product, facility, service, event or series of events. While similar to direct sales activities in that the activity is fairly closely targeted, the objectives may not concentrate on achieving an immediate sale. Various techniques can be utilised to create awareness of products and to encourage existing customers to purchase at some time in the future.

INDIRECT SALES ACTIVITIES

The operator will offer a variety of products and benefits to captive customers, and while customers are often made aware of standard items for example, the room rate or restaurant availability, many operators appear quite shy in informing customers of all available services. Menus are hidden or only displayed in the restaurant, the availability of private rooms for small parties in restaurants is not 'advertised', the opportunity for larger organisations to book out a complete leisure facility is not broadcast.

However, many operators do undertake very effective indirect sales activity, taking every opportunity to inform customers of all opportunities. An example of this would be menus in lifts, and reminders of special evening meals left in bedrooms.

INDIRECT PROMOTIONAL ACTIVITIES

Promotion is concerned with increasing the awareness of products among customers, and there exist many opportunities for hospitality operators to further indirectly promote their products. A considerable amount of indirect promotion can be undertaken by the staff in the day-to-day conversations they have with guests. Additionally, the direct effective promotion of one particular product or facility may positively enhance other services and facilities the operator provides.

In-house sales and promotional activities are not just concerned with immediately increasing sales, but also assisting longer term business. The activities will vary in approach and style. While the differentiation between the approaches is fairly fine, by analysing and identifying the aims and objectives, the operator will be able to target activities more effectively.

Basic methods of in-house selling and promotion

In-house advertising

The majority of hospitality operators utilise some form of in-house advertising to increase customers' awareness of the full range of products, services and facilities. Such advertising can take a variety of forms including: menus, food and beverage lists, tent cards, facility lists located in bedrooms, posters, messages on key cards, receipts, personal letters to guests, display boards and messages left on in-house video and television facilities.

The style and scale of such advertising is obviously dependent on the type of hospitality unit. Operators at the luxury end of the market will often keep advertising to a minimum – preferring a 'soft-sell' approach, while operators of more rapid turnover units will commonly go for a harder sell, blitzing customers with advertising that is often brightly coloured and attempts to demand the attention. Whatever the scale of the activity, the operator seeks to ensure that customers are aware of the range of products and their associated benefits.

In one city centre hotel I stayed at recently, I received a letter from the restaurant manager offering me the opportunity to 'relax' with a 'free' half bottle of wine if I utilised the hotel's restaurant that evening. (I had not made a table reservation when I checked in.)

In-house advertising can be a relatively low cost but effective way of both increasing awareness and assisting sales. Similar to external advertising, such material should be professional, clear and concise. However, advertising is impersonal, and while attempts are often made to 'personalise' some of these activities, they should be backed up with personal sales activity.

Personal sales activities

Staff should perform a vital role in promoting and increasing sales, and no amount of positive advertising, displays, merchandising and promotion will work if front-line sales staff, in particular, adversely affect sales by poor service or lack of knowledge.

Although affected by the style of operation and the type of customer, the scope for such activity is considerable in the majority of hospitality units, for instance:

- The hotel receptionist has the opportunity when the guest arrives to: upgrade the room; suggest a meal in the restaurant; order an early morning paper; organise room service.
- The food service person has the opportunity to: increase the food order by the positive description and offering of 'side orders'; sell a pre-dinner drink, wine with the meal or liqueur by utilising product knowledge skills.
- The bar person has the opportunity to increase beverage sales by: offering a speciality drink or cocktail; describing a new item stocked.

- The conference organiser has the opportunity to increase product utilisation by: offering to enhance the service by the provision of additional product.

Naturally, there exist limitations on the degree to which such selling activities can take place, and some operators train staff to repeatedly offer additional products. Fast-food operators utilise this technique as do many chain restaurants. In units with less rapid turnover, the accent is on increasing sales through a positive customer care approach. Success in increasing in-house sales will depend on the staff involved.

SUMMARY

You have seen that there exist a variety of approaches operators can utilise to increase sales with the appropriate planning. Both indirect and direct methods should be considered in relation to the style of customers and the unit. All operators possess opportunities to increase sales volume; their differing approach to this important element of marketing and sales is outlined in the next section.

RELATION TO THE VARIOUS SECTORS OF THE INDUSTRY

The hospitality industry consists of a variety of operators. While common factors and activities do exist, the type of operation will dictate the methods of in-house sales techniques utilised.

Commonly, all operators will have customers entering their premises, and all customers will hopefully make a purchase – it is the operator's role to ease the difficulties involved in this process.

The fast-food operator will utilise completely different techniques to the five-star hotel, concentrating on sharp, punchy, point-of-sale material assisted by staff trained in 'selling-up' techniques. Harder techniques have to be utilised when the customer's time is limited. The degree to which selling is pushed is often related to this time factor. Resident guests, be they relaxing over a meal or using overnight accommodation, will respond more positively to a softer, more personal technique.

Whatever the style of the operation, postive in-house selling will contain elements of effective planning, systematic approach, method selection, staff training and staff motivation. This last consideration is one of the most important. Staff training and motivation is dealt with in the final section within this chapter.

THE CONTRACT CATERING SECTOR

In-house activity is targeted at:

- Front of house/counter merchandising designed to increase sales on particular products or items.
- In-company advertising.
- Promotional activities with themed days.
- Promotional activities related to particular products run in conjunction with suppliers.

Unless the contract caterer has a monopoly, in-house sales activity is designed to maintain customer interest, satisfy these customers and the main employer, and increase overall sales volume.

THE HOTEL SECTOR

In-house activity is designed to:

- Encourage customers to utilise the unit's other or additional facilities.
- Increase sales volume in relation to food and beverage items.
- Create awareness of other units within a company.
- Create increased sales of other particular merchandised products.
- Contain customers within the unit in respect of purchase behaviour.

THE RESTAURANT SECTOR

Due to the concentration of food and beverages, activities are aimed at:

- Increasing overall sales volume.
- Developing future business by the in-house promotion of special events and 'offers'.

THE LICENSED TRADE SECTOR

Activities will be targeted at:

- Merchandising, promotion and sales of beverages.
- Promotion of future events.
- Increasing the level of utilisation of any other facility.

SUMMARY

Operators will have to utilise methods that are appropriate to their customers and their style of operation. Basic methods were outlined in the previous section and the following two sections look in more detail at the elements of campaigns and merchandising.

IN-HOUSE CAMPAIGNS AND PROMOTIONS

The importance of increasing sales volume by effective in-house selling and promotion has already been stated. This section will concentrate in more detail on the various approaches and methods for in-house sales and promotional campaigns.

The word 'campaign' suggests a systematic approach to such activities, accompanied by clearly defined aims and objectives. Given the appropriate time and skills, operators will undertake activities based on this approach whether it be reactive, that is, to alter demand, or proactive, in that it attempts to alter customer behaviour in respect of new products or potential demand. Such campaigns are not solely the prerogative of large organisations, and many small businesses conduct highly successful in-house campaigns and promotions.

In-house sales is often seen as the opportunity to discount certain products and facilities in a reaction to competition or decreased demand. Discounting is only one element of a package of in-house sales and promotion methods, and is usually a fairly drastic one to undertake. It is also difficult at times to separate in-house and external activities, as operators may also make use of external advertising and sales activity to promote in-house products, services or facilities. In-house sales and promotion activities can range from national campaigns to attempts to promote and sell one particular product or item.

THE IDENTIFICATION, PLANNING AND IMPLEMENTATION OF IN-HOUSE PROMOTION AND SALES

There are two basic types of approach to in-house promotion and sales: problem solving and problem avoidance. The first approach is often characterised by reactions to changes in demand, increased competition and the identification of product sales declines; while the second approach is often characterised by strategies to develop new markets or increased sales.

This is a rather simplistic view of such actions, and there exist other, more complex, reasons and approaches. However, it is worth exploring both approaches in more detail.

PROBLEM-SOLVING IN-HOUSE SALES AND PROMOTIONS

In this situation the operator has identified a particular problem associated with product sales and facility utilisation. Such problems could include:

- an overall decline in sales;
- an overall decline in customer numbers;
- an increase in competition;
- a decline in demand by certain of the operation's key markets;
- the identification of customer resistance to alterations in product line or price;
- the identification that, while similar competitions are operating successfully, the particular unit is experiencing slow sales;
- an overall decline in sales volume, that is, average spend per head;
- the poor utilisation of a facility, service or product within the unit, despite sound overall demand for other of the unit's products;
- a decline in demand for a particular unit of a company while other units are performing well.

It would be wrong to suggest that by solely increasing in-house promotional and sales activity, the problem would be solved. The accurate identification of the sales problem remains the primary consideration. For instance, overall decline in sales could be a result of wider economic factors, as was apparent in the early 1990s.

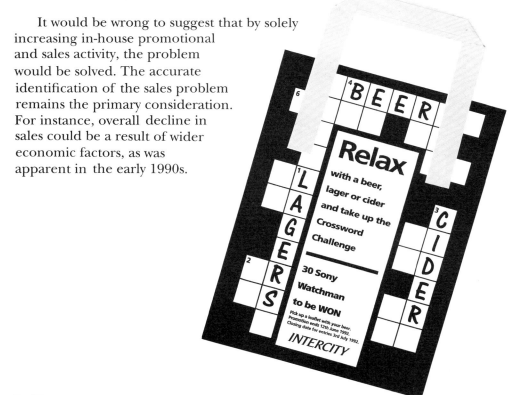

Fig. 6.2

IN-HOUSE PROMOTION CAMPAIGN FOR INTER-CITY. CARRIER BAGS ARE GIVEN AWAY WITH FOOD AND DRINK PURCHASES

In Chapter 2, reference was made to the external factors that may affect a business's performance. However, the operator will still have customers who it targeted appropriately who can affect positive sales volume.

Alterations in demand may occur rapidly, leaving the operator ill prepared to deal with the problem, which will often result in rather negative responses, such as cost cutting, quality reduction and staff losses. However unfortunate such reactions are, they are, at times, the only realistic approach.

The operator will wish not only to identify the particular problem or problems, but also identify the most cost-effective solution. *In times of recession the relatively low cost of positive in-house sales and promotional activity in relation to other sales activity remains an important consideration for hard-pressed companies.*

PROBLEM-AVOIDANCE IN-HOUSE PROMOTION AND SALES

In this situation the operator is looking to promotional and sales activities to provide not only benefits in respect of increased sales volume, but also to provide on-going analysis of business and market trends. Such activities are investigative in addition to being speculative. Operators may wish to:

- promote the sales of particular facilities or products;
- obtain feedback from customers on a facility or product;
- investigate the reasons for increased demand;
- create a public relations opportunity;
- improve customer satisfaction;
- investigate the potential demand for a new product, facility or service;
- promote increased utilisation of a service or facility which, while enjoying sound demand, has the scope for further sales;
- undertake seasonal promotional activities;
- create increased customer awareness of a future planned event, product or service.

With all of the above, the operator is looking to the future, not reacting solely to past levels of business. For instance, a hotel may be planning a new leisure facility, gourmet club or special weekend packages; a restaurant may be considering alterations to the standard menu; while a conference and business centre may be seeking to establish the range of facilities such business will require in the future. In addition to the normal marketing activities, operators will seek to utilise existing customers for obtaining future marketing information.

In conclusion, there exist two general approaches to in-house promotion and sales. Both have their advantages and disadvantages, and both, if utilised correctly, will assit the operator in not only identifying an existing or potential problem, but also in identifying the most appropriate method to overcome them.

THE SELECTION OF METHODS

Similar to the majority of other marketing and sales activity, the operator seeks to utilise methods that will:

- most cost effectively achieve the aims of the activity; and
- match the style of customer and operation.

A hotel may decide to promote its restaurant or eating facilities, and activities could include additional in-house advertising, a check on the numbers of overnight guests who have booked a table or a written message to those who have not booked a table. Additionally, certain discounts may be offered, or offers such as a free half-bottle of wine for residents eating before 7.45 pm be promoted.

A restaurant may decide to promote a forthcoming special event, such as a 'Beaujolais evening' or '4 July celebration', and concentrate all promotional activities in-house, with posters, tent cards, reminders on bills and personal approaches to existing customers. A hotel or restaurant may also operate regular events and rely on word of mouth advertising and in-house promotion. One such example is detailed below.

Don and Samantha Horton run a busy hotel and restaurant in Devon and have achieved considerable success in positive promotional and PR activity: 'We tend not to advertise due to the high cost and questionable return. Effective sales and marketing has always been a key element of our business and not something which commenced with the recession.'

The Hortons have had particular success in operating a gourmet club for a number of years, and regular gourmet dinners attract considerable additional business. Special gourmet dinners are offered to club members approximately six times per year, which result in an average of 40 extra covers. The advertising and promotion is fairly low key; restaurant customers are made aware of the facility by a message on the menu and encouraged to provide their names and addresses for club membership. This data is entered on to a computer which assists with regular direct mail shots. Club members usually average at least two dinners per year in addition to other more regular use of the restaurant.

Other activities are undertaken to promote the restaurant and the gourmet club. Several successful charity fund-raising events have been organised. Following up one particular idea to offer a wartime menu, the Hortons wrote to the local press requesting recipes from the readers. The response was immediate: two local radio stations did 'spots' on the event, and the region's television service invited Mr Horton in to demonstrate some of the recipes. The positive media coverage of the charity events and the wartime menu resulted

(continued)

---

in a considerable amount of additional bookings, including five weddings booked from guests at one event.

'National advertising is too costly for smaller businesses like ours – the key is to select brochures and guides issued by the tourist boards which target your particular market and ones in which you can evaluate the returns.

'Nothing is more important than in-house selling. When the customer comes through the door, that's the time to show you care about them and their comfort. Staff must be trained in positive customer care and understand how this contributes to the survival of a business.'

While there existed elements of external promotion of the provision, the key factor was the in-house approach the owners undertook.

SUMMARY

All operators have opportunities for such campaigns and promotions, and while they require careful planning as activities, they are an integral part of the complete process of marketing and sales actions designed to generate profitable business.

Activities such as in-house promotions require knowledge of other sales and marketing techniques, including advertising and merchandising. This latter method is becoming increasingly recognised as a positive indirect sales method and is detailed in the next section.

THE ROLE OF MERCHANDISING

Merchandising has not traditionally been seen as an appropriate activity for increasing sales in the hospitality industry. This is especially true of the hotel and restaurant sector. Contract caterers utilise this method increasingly and in an extremely professional manner.

They recognise the part that merchandising can play in increasing sales. Other sectors' use of this method is dependent on its particular style and range of goods and services, the most common being in the layout of a bar, where the display of beverages is designed to raise awareness of the produce and create the appropriate stimulus in the customer.

DEFINITION OF MERCHANDISING
Several definitions of merchandising exist, which change dependent on the sector in which it is being used. For the hospitality industry, I believe the best definition is: non-personal promotion close to the point of sale which, by appealing to the customers' senses, assist and encourage the further profitable sale of products or goods.

Merchandising works mainly by:

- increasing the awareness of goods or products;
- increasing the accessibility of goods by preventing barriers to sales;
- appealing to customers' senses;

therefore encouraging the customers to purchase.

Similar to all sales and marketing activity, merchandising requires planning if it is to be successful, and is part of the armoury of methods available to the hospitality operator.

Its main uses by hospitality operators are:

- within bar areas – promoting the sales of beverages and food items;
- as part of food display – promoting the sales of additional food and beverage items.

PROMOTIONAL DISPLAYS

Promotional displays can form a positive part of non-personal selling within a hospitality unit. Static displays placed where they can attract interest and promote additional purchases are quite common in the industry – particularly in the hotel sector.

Hotels often utilise spare wall space for the display of retail items, unit related material, for example, gifts with the hotel's logo on, and printed material with associated products. Additionally, the hospitality unit may link with another company to jointly promote a particular product or service.

THE BASIC GUIDELINES FOR PROMOTIONAL DISPLAYS

- The display should be planned with a clear objective in mind.
- The display should be professional, informative and attractive, relating clearly to the item, product or service being promoted.
- The display should be in a location that is both safe, not liable to damage or theft and where it can activate the maximum impact.
- Displays should be changed regularly, the longer it remains *in situ*, the less the resulting demand generated by it.

EXAMPLES OF THE USE OF MERCHANDISING

The type and range of merchandising will relate to the type of customer and style of operation, and additionally to the skills operators and their staff possess related to this function. Examples of merchandising are:

- The display of particular products in a bar, restaurant or at a service counter. There exist many studies on the placing of items within a counter service or bar area, and where they will best attract a passing customer's eyes and interest – known in the industry as 'hot spots'. The aim in such display and merchandising is to fill 'cold' or 'blank' areas in an attempt to stimulate customers into unplanned purchases.

- The display of products for sale related to the establishment, for example, souvenirs, items of clothing, jewellery and other gifts.

Many hotels, motorway service restaurants and some themed restaurants utilise such merchandising in an attempt to generate additional revenue.

SUMMARY

The hospitality industry possesses growing opportunities for the generation of additional sales by the use of merchandising techniques. For certain operators providing high-cost luxury accommodation, such merchandising will often be fairly low key, while for operators with fast turn-round facilities, the approach will be more aggressive.

Sensitive merchandising which reinforces other sales methods can provide important contributions to sales revenue, and it is a method which will increase over the coming years.

The final section in this chapter will detail the importance of staff involvement, training and motivation in relation to in-house promotion and sales.

STAFF TRAINING AND MOTIVATION

All the staff within a unit are, or should be, involved in the selling process directly or indirectly. It is the responsibility of management to see that such involvement takes place through careful planning, training and evaluation of results. For an individual to increase in-house sales, he or she requires certain basic knowledge, skills and attributes:

Knowledge of the products and services, not just of the particular area or department the individual works directly in, but of the whole operation. This aspect was dealt with in more detail in Chapter 5.

Skills are concerned not just with the tasks and skills involved in a particular job, for example, serving wine or booking in a guest, but also communication skills, such as the greeting of clients and complaint handling.

These first two considerations are possibly the easiest to ensure with the appropriate selection of staff and basic training. The last consideration, that of attributes, is more complex and involves the operator in a variety of activities.

Personal attributes. To sell effectively, individuals must have confidence not only in themselves, but also the unit itself and its products and services. They must consider themselves part of a team where the need to increase sales coincides with positive customer care practices.

All three considerations are concerned with affecting the behaviour of staff, providing them with the skills, confidence and appropriate attitude to maximise on sales opportunities.

ASPECTS OF MOTIVATION

Staff will be more successful in increasing in-house sales if they are provided with:

- knowledge of the products and services;
- practical skills to ensure the satisfactory completion of tasks;
- customer care skills enabling them to deal positively with all situations;
- personal skills to increase their own confidence and self-esteem.

All of these should be a standard part of ongoing training within the unit. By providing staff, both individually and as a team, the opportunity to increase knowledge and skills, the operator lays a solid framework for positive selling.

As the majority of sales and marketing is designed to create a positive link between external customers and hospitality products and services, so in-house selling is concerned with bridging the sales gap between existing customers and additional products, services and facilities the hospitality unit offers. Training is then best targeted at methods and activities which bridge the sales gap, raising awareness of products and services and motivating a change in customer buying behaviour.

TARGETING TRAINING

Hospitality operators involved in positive in-house selling will utilise a variety of training methods including:

- induction training;
- product training;
- team training, including brainstorming for ideas;
- customer care training.

MOTIVATING STAFF TO SELL

If the individual or team have sound product knowledge, effective skills and the appropriate personal attributes, they then have a sound base for increasing sales. Various methods of further motivating staff are utilised within the industry including:

- awards: employee of the month, merit stars, etc;
- prizes: cash or gifts given to individuals or teams;
- bonuses: cash bonuses linked to individual or team performance;
- company shares: given to employees in recognition of overall company performance.

While the industry is a service one, it is justifiable on both moral and business grounds to provide such incentives. However, there do exist problems that can demotivate staff. The best method of motivation is one which shares any benefits to all staff in a fair and open manner, based on some form of equal evaluation process measuring target sales against actual sales. The increase in the use of technology in recording sales has helped this process.

The hospitality operator will need to plan not only the in-house campaign, including the training and methods utilised, but also the form of evaluation process enabling the appropriate reward of the personnel involved.

The management must seek not only to create the correct physical environment but also an environment where staff have personal pride and commitment to the unit.

METHODS OF TRAINING

It is important to target training in two directions:

- at staff with highest level of customer contact and, therefore, greatest opportunity to affect sales;
- at areas, facilities, products and services which possess the greatest opportunity for increased sales.

A variety of methods exist including:

- *Team training* where small groups of employees are brought together for either general training related to particular skills, or for specific training related to such aspects as complaint handling, increasing a product's sales, or for a forthcoming promotion.
- *Team brainstorming* where small groups of staff from key areas meet to brainstorm ideas for improving customer care and increasing sales. Additionally, the group may discuss and report on factors that affect the potential increase in sales.
- *Individual training* where employees receive written briefs, learning packs, videos or aspects related to the promotion of sales. (Due to increased pressure on operators, this method is gaining in popularity.)

The company or organisation may utilise external trainers or their own staff, such as departmental heads or experienced sales personnel, to design and deliver such training. In addition to direct targeted training, organisations may identify the need to provide attitudinal training, that is, training related to increasing staff's understanding of the part attitude plays in in-house selling and customer care.

AREA OR FACILITY TRAINING

Here the operator is concerned with ensuring that staff have the appropriate knowledge and skills to promote a given area or particular products and services, such as the restaurant, accommodation or bar.

Training is usually conducted by the departmental head. Elements of other methods may be utilised, and while this is traditionally delivered at induction, it should in reality be an ongoing element of staff training and motivation.

SUMMARY

Staff form what some marketing personnel refer to as the fifth 'P', an addition to the four P's of the marketing mix. All staff should be directly or indirectly involved in selling and promotion, and operators need to ensure they possess the appropriate knowledge, skills and attributes to achieve these aims.

As with many other elements of the marketing and sales function, it is the staff themselves who will deliver the end product, and their role in increasing in-house sales should not be underestimated.

CHAPTER REVIEW

Hospitality operators cannot rely solely on external sales and marketing activities to attract customers through their doors and so they should assist the potential profitability of the business.

Once captive, the customer is an additional sales opportunity in that, utilising appropriate methods, the staff can encourage further sales, further increasing the sales volume. Such activities are not necessarily expensive in relation to their potential outcome. This capture of additional income is dependent on a variety of factors, such as positive planning, methods, training and incentives.

Personal selling can be assisted by non-personal promotional activities all designed to raise awareness in the client of the total range of products, services and related benefits, thereby assisting a positive change in customer buying behaviour.

The placing before staff of incentives to sell is just as important as providing incentives to customers to purchase additional products or services. Appropriate staff training and incentives linked to a positive customer care programme will increase customer satisfaction and repeat business.

The methods utilised to encourage in-house sales will vary from unit to unit. However, all units, regardless of their style, possess opportunities to increase profitable sales volume. Similar to all sales and marketing activities, costs should be considered in relation to both forecasted and actual outcomes.

Positive in-house selling is, then, a vital part of the hospitality operator's activities in profitable sales. As part of a positive customer care programme, it builds upon the energies and costs related to initial sales and marketing activity.

KEY POINTS

- Positive in-house selling is concerned with both increased average spend per head and customer satisfaction.
- In-house selling embraces both non-personal and personal selling.
- By increasing sales volume, the operator will assist overall profit levels at relatively low cost.
- In-house selling should be approached systematically with a clear plan of who does what and how.
- All staff should be involved, assisting sales in other departments.
- Staff should be trained and provided with incentives.
- All hospitality operators can increase sales volume by positive in-house selling.

QUESTIONS

- Describe the contribution which effective in-house selling can make to sales volume.
- List four methods of in-house selling and identify for each an appropriate target.
- List the factors a hospitality operator should consider when planning increased in-house selling.
- Explain how merchandising could increase sales in a restaurant or bar.
- Discuss the importance of effective staff training in relation to improving in-house sales.
- Identify the factors a hospitality operator should consider when planning a specific event promotion.

BOOK SUMMARY

This text has provided you with an introduction to both the theory and practice of marketing and sales activities. Commencing with an outline of the industry and the relevance of marketing and sales for the organisations, further sections identified and explained the various methods or actions operators undertake to *identify and satisfy customers profitably*.

Throughout the book, the importance of planning control and evaluation was stressed; although this may appear to indicate that marketing and sales is an academic discipline, the reality is that such activity is concerned with people.

Marketing is seen by some to be a science, an aspect I would agree with. Planning, research analysis and evaluation all form part of the marketing process. There are uncertainties with marketing information collected, such data is at best a forecast of needs, demands, threats and opportunities. However, it does provide operators with increasingly accurate indicators on which to base sales and promotional activity. If marketing is a science, then it can be separated from the sales function, which perhaps is more an art.

Sales activities and actions, while being based upon quantifiable research, relies additionally on the personal skills and attributes of the personnel involved. Such personnel, whether they be marketing and sales directors of large companies, unit sales managers, owners, proprietors or operative staff, are all involved in indirect activities with the most important person – the customer.

Experienced, professional and caring staff in day-to-day contact with the customer are the practitioners of the real art of marketing and sales, that is, effective customer care.

Companies who undertake effective identification of customer needs and demands will be thwarted in their attempts to maintain and develop profitable business if the deliverers of their plans, that is, the staff, are poorly trained and motivated.

No marketing plan however sophisticated will make up for poor quality service or indifferent customer care. Yet positive customer care will often overcome inadequacies in a company's marketing efforts.

It must be recognised that marketing and sales activities cannot function by themselves. They form an integral part of the business alongside successful operational management, budget and cost control and effective resource management.

The science and function of market research, advertising, selling skills, and promotional campaigns are all aspects along with others within the text that could usefully be extended. This is in part achieved by the inclusion of the exercises and assignments in Appendix A. Whether you are a student being introduced to this fascinating subject for the first time, or a hospitality operator with an interest in this area, completion of these assignments will enhance your understanding of marketing and sales and provide you with increased confidence and skills.

Marketing and sales practitioners will often identify the need to take risks in planned activities. Such risk taking is one of the enjoyable aspects of marketing and sales. Not every action will be a success – although by sound research and planning the chances of success are increased.

Effective marketing and sales should be concerned with *actions and outcomes*. Having an understanding of the complexities of consumer behaviour and market research variables, while important, should not detract the individual from concentrating on practical, cost-effective activities which clearly assist the generation of positive customer care and profitable business.

I hope you have enjoyed both reading and working through this book. It has been successful if it has provided you with a sound base on which to build further skills and expertise.

APPENDIX A:
MARKETING AND SALES ASSIGNMENTS AND EXERCISES

INTRODUCTION

The exercises and assignments detailed in this section could be utilised in a variety of ways:

- As individual and group exercises alongside related questions (provided at the end of each chapter).
- As exercises for individuals using the text within their studies.
- As examples of written work for either course assessment purposes or to provide written evidence of knowledge and skills.
- Completed assignments could be made use of by individuals to enhance their curriculum vitae or record of achievement folder.
- As practical assignments based upon the unit they work in. It should be noted that there exists no one correct solution for the assignments.

  Other points on the use of exercises and assignments:

- The exercises and assignments relate to particular chapters and sections within the text. As this is an introductory text, readers should turn to other reference material where appropriate.
- The assignments are designed to act as individual pieces of work and as an overall assignment. If all the assignments are undertaken, it is recommended that the student identifies one particular establishment or company that will agree to a more in-depth study. There are obvious advantages and disadvantages to this approach. By concentrating on one particular unit or company, the student will reduce the overall workload and have the experience of analysing a unit's performance in depth. By utilising different units for each assignment, the student will gain wider experience of the varying approaches to sales and marketing problems. Not all the assignments have to be completed to make up the package – only choose ones relevant to your studies or work situation.
- If the assignments are to be utilised for course assessment, certification, validation as part of a curriculum vitae or as part of a record of achievement, then consideration should be given to the professional

presentation of the work – there are text books and guides to presentation in most public libraries.

- If assignments are undertaken by a group, then careful consideration should be given to the distribution of the responsibilities within the group, either by the tutor, manager, trainer or group itself.
- I have not indicated an approximate time for completion of assignments as this depends on the way the work will be undertaken. However, setting a period limit with target dates is an essential part of sales and marketing activity, so apply this rule to your work.
- For managers, trainers or tutors using this text, I would advise discussion with the trainee at the outset to clarify objectives, overall content and presentation.

FINAL POINTS

I have used many of these assignments in both training and tutoring situations, with young students, adult groups and supervisors with sales and marketing skills. It is my experience that the careful use of practically based assignments provides students with a variety of learning opportunities not available in more traditional training and teaching situations. Additionally, because the assignments are designed for use in the workplace, creating real solutions to business needs, they hold particular relevance. The exercises can be utilised in group work or brainstorming exercises.

Below is an outline plan which places the assignments in relevant order and identifies the area they cover.

ASSIGNMENT PLAN

If you decide to complete all or a number of the assignments based on one particular unit, it is recommended you follow the sequence outlined below. For a hospitality employee this would allow comprehensive analysis of the company and promote possible ideas for business development; for a student this would allow the integration of the various disciplines introduced throughout the text.

It should be remembered that each assignment is designed to be 'free standing', and if only one is utilised there exists the opportunity to expand the brief in a variety of ways.

ASSIGNMENT		MAIN AREAS COVERED
No. 1	Product review	Review and analysis of the operator's current product range
No. 2	Analysis of performance	Analysis of actual performance
No. 3	Identification of customer needs	The making use of customer feedback to identify future activity
No.4	Sales methods review	Analysis of current methods and effectiveness of sales activity
No. 5	Evaluating product knowledge and customer care	Conduction of a quality 'audit'
No. 6	In-house selling and promotion	Analysis of methods to increase sales volume
No. 7	Marketing and sales plan	Combination of elements to produce an overall effective plan

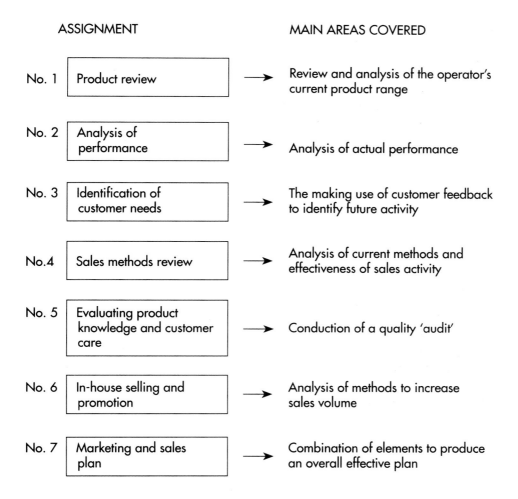

CHAPTER 1:
INTRODUCTION TO HOSPITALITY MARKETING

This chapter provided you with a background to the hospitality industry in connection with general sales and marketing activities. It outlined the relevance of marketing and sales to the industry and identified the importance of understanding the complex relationships between markets, customers, companies and their products. The differing styles of approach to marketing and sales was identified and the specific role and responsibilities of sales personnel was explained.

The exercises and assignments within this section are designed to further this introduction of the role and importance of marketing and sales.

Specifically they ask you to investigate in more detail:

● The range of products an operator offers.
● The selection of appropriate marketing and sales activity for three contrasting hospitality units.
● An outline of responsibilities for a sales and marketing person.

ASSIGNMENT No. 1:

REVIEWING AN OPERATOR'S PRODUCT RANGE

After agreement with the operator of your choice, complete the following:

● Compile a list of the range of products, that is, facilities, services and goods, the operator currently provides. You are advised to select a unit where a range of 'products' are available, for example, rooms, conference facilities, functions.
● Describe briefly each product in terms of content, for example, weekend break, and identify: the current market, that is, the user, and the potential market.

This product review is designed for students or employees to commence investigating in detail a particular unit. Its completion will allow you to gain a more thorough understanding of the business, how it operates, what it offers and who are its main customers. A consultant offering marketing services to a client will often commence an assignment in this way.

EXERCISE No. 1:

IDENTIFYING SUITABLE APPROACHES TO MARKETING AND SALES ACTIVITY

For each of the three businesses described below, compile a report outlining:

● The marketing and sales approach that would be most effective in relation to maintaining and improving business.
● A list of marketing and sales activities on which the operator should concentrate.

THE GREENHEAD INN AND RESTAURANT

This inn is situated on the outskirts of a busy commercial centre, within an area which includes residential housing, a country park and several tourist attractions. Facilities include two bars, serving the local and tourist trade with drinks and high-quality bar snacks. The 60-seater restaurant is open for both lunch and dinner and has a growing reputation for 'up market' type meals. Additionally, there is a function room accommodating 100 people for a sit down meal and a modern play area for children. Present customer base is quite mixed, although the inn is not heavily utilised by people between 18 and 24 years of age.

THE WELBECK LODGE HOTEL

This newly opened hotel situated in a rural area has 25 bedrooms, a restaurant, bar, fitness room, swimming pool, tennis courts, two functions rooms and three conference/seminar rooms. Road access is very good. The hotel has extensive grounds, fishing rights on a nearby river, and aims to serve a mixed clientele of residential conferences, weekend breaks and individual visitors attracted to the area.

THE CUFFLEY RESTAURANT

This restaurant specialises in high-quality lunches and dinners provided over five days per week and Thursday, Friday and Saturday evenings. Situated in the high street of a busy tourist market town, it offers mainly salad and 'healthy' type lunches. In the evenings, it operates an international type menu with a range of regional dishes. Adjoining the restaurant is a delicatessen offering a wide range of specialist food items. Daytime customers purchasing items from the delicatessen often take lunch in the restaurant, which can accommodate approximately 60 people. The customer base is a mix of shoppers and tourists at lunch times and dinners.

EXERCISE NO. 2:
ROLES AND RESPONSIBILITIES OF SALES PERSONNEL

The selection of appropriately skilled and qualified personnel is of great importance for all positions. As the position of a business alters, so too does its demand for staff. The opening of a premises poses particular challenges for sales and marketing personnel, especially if the unit is an independent one and lacks the customer awareness of its services and facilities.

The individual working with the management will have to obtain new business, starting from scratch. The responsibilities within the few months prior to opening and during the first year will be different if the unit had been trading for some time.

The Fairbridge Hotel is close to opening. Situated close to a busy industrial estate and large city it has 60 bedrooms, a bar, restaurant function room (accommodating 150 people) and four seminar rooms. As general manager you wish to appoint a sales and marketing assistant who will concentrate on obtaining appropriate business for the hotel. Compile an outline job description for the position, identifying the main responsibilities of the post and list the main activities the individual will undertake within the first year of appointment.

CHAPTER 2:

MARKETING PLANNING AND STRATEGY

Similar to all business activities, marketing requires effective planning to assist the probability of success. Hospitality operators will utilise long-term planning with specific aims and objectives to maximise revenue. These strategic plans are founded upon market information which, when used appropriately, will provide the hospitality operator with a firm base on which to operate the business effectively and develop future sales opportunities.

The exercises and assignment outlined are designed to allow you opportunity to:

- Experience the complexity of effective evaluation and planning in relation to marketing and sales activities.
- Conduct a detailed business review and analysis.
- Prepare a report based upon a business analysis with accompanying statistical material.
- Prepare an outline action plan for launching a new hotel.

ASSIGNMENT NO. 2:

REVIEWING PERFORMANCE AND CUSTOMER MIX

For a hospitality unit of your choice or the one you are utilising for all the assignments, complete the following:

- For each of the main operating areas within the unit, for example, accommodation, bar, restaurant or conference facility, identify by investigation and research the following:
    - the current overall level of business, that is, occupancy or utilisation;
    - the level of business in respect of different trading periods, that is, by month, week, day or time;
    - current client mix, that is, business, tourist, families;
    - by reference to information available, the source of the business, that is, the percentage of business clients on account; the percentage on tourists on package deals; and the percentage of families attracted by advertising.
- Report on your findings utilising graphs where appropriate.
- Identify any particular gaps in occupancy or activity and briefly outline proposals for improving business.

This is a fairly extensive assignment and will require access to a variety of staff within the unit. It is designed to allow you to carry out a fairly detailed review. It is suggested that if you plan to complete a number of the assignments based on one particular unit, then this assignment should be tackled first.

Exercise No. 3:

TAKING A HOTEL TO ITS MARKET

The Wyatt Hotel Group

The operators of a small but growing hotel group are close to completing the building of their sixth hotel, situated close to motorway and rail links and a busy industrial centre.

The hotel group aims to attract mainly business and conference trade. Competition in the area exists with hotels from all the larger hotel groups within a 20-mile radius.

The company's strategy is to provide personalised quality service, with prices slightly higher than the rates charged by the larger groups.

The company targets the small- to medium-size conference market, the business traveller, local trade for its restaurant at weekends, and the up-market speciality weekend market.

As the newly appointed sales and conference manager, your first task is to outline your initial activities in generating advance sales for the hotel. The manager has asked you to complete an outline marketing plan in order to:

- raise awareness of the hotel within targeted market segments;
- raise awareness of the hotel with appropriate travel and booking agencies;
- attract appropriate local business clients.

All of these could also be covered in an outline action plan, which summarises the activities and identifies the particular aims of each activity.

Exercise No. 4:

THE CONCEPT OF BRANDING

Pastiera Restaurants

The owners of this chain of Italian restaurants have approached you to advise them on the advantages of standardising their outlets. At present, they operate eight outlets across a region. All offer similar types of food and beverages and operate under a resident manager. All the units are extremely successful; however, the owners are keen to standardise menus and style with the aim of increasing the number of units considerably.

What they seek from you is a brief report in respect of the advantages of branding their outlets and what type of local and regional sales and marketing activity would be required. You could complete this either as a written report or as a presentation.

Remember that all the owners require is an outline report. It would be on the effectiveness of this report or presentation whether they employ you as a consultant to action your recommendations.

CHAPTER 3:
IDENTIFYING CUSTOMER NEEDS

Chapter 3 described the importance of identifying customer needs. Without careful and continuing analysis of the existing and potential clients, the hospitality operator lacks information on which to base future business and development. You will see that identifying needs is not just about looking at existing customers, but also at other potential customers and markets.

The exercises and assignments outlined are designed to allow you the opportunity to:

- design an appropriate guest comment card;
- consider the mechanisms for the analysis, evaluation and response to customer feedback;
- consider in more depth the sources of market information an operator could utilise to assist decision making.

ASSIGNMENT No. 3:
OBTAINING CUSTOMER FEEDBACK

For a hospitality unit of your choice, complete the following:

- Design and compile a guest comment card soliciting views on how the unit could improve its service or facilities.
- Explain how best this comment card should be distributed to guests, and what form of incentive should be offered to encourage its completion and return (if any).
- Explain how you recommend responding to the comments received – to the guests and in terms of informing staff.
- Consider and report on any other ways the operator can obtain feedback from existing and past customers.

Exercise No. 5:

Analysis, evaluation and utilisation of customer feedback

Pine Lodge Hotel

The Pine Lodge is a two- to three-star medium price range hotel situated close to a motorway junction. With 70 bedrooms, a bar, restaurant and small meeting room facility, it services mainly commercial/business markets with an annual occupancy level of 62 per cent.

This is a relatively modest hotel with emphasis being on reasonable quality facilities and friendly service. Owned and operated by a family for a number of years, it enjoys reasonable, if not exciting, profits and has a fairly secure market position. (Note that there exists no possibility for Travelodge to open up the road!)

As the manager (in the post for just over ten months), you have increased the feedback from guests by issuing comment cards, soliciting verbal comments and analysing complaints received by post. With a stock of over 150 comment cards, several pages of customer comments and 20 letters of complaints, you now have to consider how to make use of them. The owners, aware that you started the review, would like to see both the results and your recommendations:

Prepare a brief written report outlining the following:

- How you intend analysing the information in terms of any proposed action.
- How you intend communicating the results of your survey to staff (both negative and positive comments).
- What suggestions you have for responding to customers' written negative and positive comments to assist customer satisfaction.

Exercise No. 6:

Identifying sources of marketing information

Following your review of customer comments related to the Pine Lodge Hotel (see Exercise No. 5), the owners have now asked you to identify for them other ways of obtaining market information.

Impressed with your review of customer comments and your suggestions for the effective utilisation of them, they feel additional research is required to obtain a wider view of their business and its performance.

Concerned with the possible cost of detailed market research, they require a list of sources of market information they can readily access with you to aid decision making.

Compile a list of sources of market information appropriate to the hotel, briefly explaining the relevance of each source.

CHAPTER 4:

MARKETING AND SALES METHODS

Chapter 4 introduced some of the basic sales and marketing methods and the importance of planning and control. For individuals commencing sales and marketing activity, such methods or actions are very often their starting point. Each method identified is worthy of a text in their own right. However, for many operators an understanding of the basic principles is sufficient.

The exercises and assignment in this section are designed to give you experience in both planning and compiling solution or proposals concerned with such activities.

Assignment No. 4 requires you to conduct an in-depth review of a unit's current sales methods and activites. Normally, a marketing specialist or consultant would conduct a complete marketing audit, of which this element would be a part. Additionally, the consultant would seek to establish from the customer viewpoint the effectiveness of such activities.

Exercise No. 7 concerns a PR approach to post-business success and proposed additions, while Exercise No. 8 is concerned with the compilation of a basic press release.

ASSIGNMENT NO. 4:

MARKETING AND SALES REVIEW

For the hospitality unit of your choice, complete the following:

- Conduct a review of all the sales and marketing activities the operator currently utilises. Briefly list each activity, describing how it is undertaken and explain and report on the following: the aim of the activity; the target market; the method of evaluation. (For some units, this review could be considerable; in this case, you may be advised to concentrate either on main activities, or ones which the operator wishes to improve.)
- Present your findings in a written report, detailing your analysis of the effectiveness of activities undertaken and your recommendations for any improvements.

EXERCISE NO. 7:

THE PROMOTION OF 'PACKAGES' BY PR

As the manager of a small but increasingly successful tourist hotel and facility, you are developing range of craft and special interest packages. Designed to attract customers to your establishment in the traditionally quieter trading periods, you have been reasonably successful in attracting customers to packages that include: regional cookery with a famous chef; photography weekends; cultural heritage two-day packages in conjunction with the tourist board and three local National Trust properties; and a sewing/needlecraft three-day package.

The packages have been well supported in the past and you wish to increase the provision by adding in a 'Murder Mystery' weekend and a 'German cultural' weekend. Both of these have been identified as potential successes.

While you have an established mailing list and advertise in the appropriate specialist media, you are also keen to maximise on the PR opportunities. Compile an outline of ideas for ways of generating positive PR out of the above successful past events and planned new ones.

Exercise No. 8:

Press releases

Referring to Exercise No. 7, compile press releases suitable for sending to:

- the local press;
- specialist trade journals;
- local television/radio stations.

The press releases should follow basic guidelines for PR material. However, use your imagination in preparing material that will increase the chances of media coverage.

Chapter 5:

Sales skills and techniques

This chapter attempted to outline both the knowledge, skills and attributes required to sell effectively and how these should be related to an understanding of customer behaviour and customer care.

In many respects, the elements identified within the chapter are the most difficult to outline in a book. Selling is a very personal activity with a considerable number of psychological factors to consider.

The assignment and exercises within this section will provide you with increased confidence in your own skills and allow you to deal more effectively with the common sales challenges facing hospitality personnel. Exercise No. 9 is specifically designed for group training sessions.

ASSIGNMENT NO. 5:

EVALUATING PRODUCT KNOWLEDGE AND CUSTOMER CARE

This particular assignment is a fairly sensitive one as it asks you to conduct a survey on the end product(s) of a unit. Many operators utilise external participants or observers to provide an objective evaluation of the quality of staff, services and facilities. Consider also that hotel, pub and restaurant guides conduct similar 'investigations' on hospitality units.

Planned appropriately, conducted professionally and used correctly, such external audits can be a very effective way of obtaining additional objective views and reports on an establishment. This could include telephone enquiries to ascertain product knowledge and customer handling skills, sampling of food and beverage service and the use of accommodation facilities.

You are advised to check carefully with the operator the following before completing this assignment:

- the areas to be covered;
- the nature and scope of the 'investigation';
- the covering of any costs incurred;
- the nature and content of any report.

Complete a structured audit on the particular unit, and utilise a variety of methods to ascertain the depth of product knowledge and the quality of customer care.

EXERCISE NO. 9:

SELLING SKILLS (GROUP ACTIVITY)

This exercise is designed as a group activity and will need to be planned by a trainer or lecturer. The exercise takes individuals through a particular sales situation, allowing the opportunity for role play, group discussion and team learning.

The situation is of a face-to-face sales meeting between a representative of a medium-sized city centre hotel and a prospective client. Trainers/lecturers could, of course, adapt the exercise to other types of establishments. However, the objective should be to take the trainee or student through the various stages of the selling process.

It is suggested that the training exercise be conducted in the following way:

- An introduction to the theory of the three stages of the selling process.
- The distribution of individual briefing notes.

- An explanation of the process:
  - trainees/students should be given a time limit both to read particular briefs, and to conduct the meeting;
  - following the meeting, they should report back with each party outlining briefly what information was obtained or, more importantly, not obtained.

  Both parties should be encouraged to explain how they 'felt' about the meeting (accepting its slightly false nature) and whether they thought they were successful.
  - Key points could be identified on a flip chart, board or on an overhead projector.
  - The conclusion should be a re-emphasis on both the problems associated with face-to-face selling and the importance of utilising this stage approach.

This type of training exercise works particularly well, and it is one I have used with a variety of groups. The important factor is the experience learned, not the degree to which some individuals can act! Trainers may wish not to show details of the briefing notes to the opposite party.

BRIEFING NOTES 1: HOTEL SALESPERSON

As sales representative of a three-star city centre hotel you are meeting today Mr Smythe, who you know is a senior director of a local company with approximately 250 employees. The initial enquiry was to look over your training room facilities and discuss the possible booking of a series of training courses.

Your manager is keen that you obtain the business as there has been a reduction in demand for the meeting facilities within the hotel. You have never met Mr Smythe before.

BRIEFING NOTE 2: MR SMYTHE, DIRECTOR, POWER TOOLS LTD

Your company, with over 250 employees, is joining with a sister organisation to operate a series of one-day training courses for supervisors and junior managers. There would be a maximum of 15 delegates for each course, and you are considering a programme of approximately 12 courses across a six-month period.

You are keen to obtain a reasonable price due to the level of custom you are bringing, and you are aware that the hotel, like others in the city, needs the business. You personally favour this particular hotel. However, your sister organisation has an alternative which it favours.

NOTES

This exercise also relates to the skills required for face-to-face selling, and trainers may wish to emphasise the aspects of the stages of the selling process and elements of personalised selling.

Exercise No. 10:

Improving customer care

Falmouth Green Hotel and Restaurant

As a director of the 50-bedroomed Falmouth Green Hotel and Restaurant, you are adapting your establishment to match the increasingly discerning clientele who use the hotel. With a small but loyal local staff, you have always prided yourself on the friendliness and informality of your establishment. However, you have realised that customers are expecting a more 'professional' type of service and care. Guest comment cards and comments received directly from customers, coupled with a slight increase in the number of complaints and your perception of a need for an attitudinal change, have all reinforced your feelings that you need to address the topic of customer care.

Reluctant to seek assistance from external agencies, you have conducted some desk research, reading several articles and books on the subject. Now you have tasked yourself to achieve two initial objectives:

- To conduct some form of research into the actual standards of care received by customers.
- To compile a priority list of areas within the hotel which require targeting first.

As director of the hotel, compile a brief report for the owners outlining the following:

- The methods you propose to use in order to evaluate customer perceptions of standards.
- The key areas within the hotel that you consider to be a priority, explaining briefly the reasons behind each key area listed.

Chapter 6:

The concept and practice of in-house selling

In-house selling has often been seen as an activity most appropriate to the hotel sector. However, as you have seen, the majority of hospitality units can and do utilise such activities to further promote awareness of products, services and facilities and encourage increased customer spend.

The assignment and exercises within this section are designed to illustrate common problems and situations within the industry. The aim of the tasks is to provide students with the opportunity to explore particular selling challenges and identify outline solutions.

Assignment No. 6 allows you to continue with the full review of one particular establishment, while Exercise No. 11 requires you to prepare written arguments for increasing staff training in respect of sales against pressure to actually reduce staff.

Exercise No. 12 poses quite a different problem concentrating on a tourist facility where the main business is not catering, yet there needs to be an increase in customer spend and utilisation.

ASSIGNMENT NO. 6:

IDENTIFYING EFFECTIVE PRACTICE

For a hospitality unit of your choice, or the unit you are utilising for all the assignments, complete the following:

- undertake a review of the current techniques and activities utilised to increase in-house sales;
- prepare a written report for the manager identifying: the range of activities currently undertaken (briefly); and your proposals for improvement or adaptation of those activities to further increase sales;
- identify with the manager one particular product, service, facility or event and outline in detail an in-house sales campaign.

The last item could be taken as an assignment in its own right and extended to include the design of appropriate posters or advertising material.

EXERCISE NO. 11:

SOLVING A DECREASE IN DEMAND BY IMPROVING IN-HOUSE SALES

BRAMPTON LODGE

Brampton Lodge is a privately owned, three-star, 60 bedroomed country house and conference hotel close to a busy industrial centre. The lodge has been open for some five years and has built up a reasonable business from both local and national clientele.

The hotel is set in its own grounds and has a bar, restaurant, leisure and conference facilities. Occupancy levels on accommodation have averaged about 65 per cent across the year, with the average spend per head (1991 prices) as follows:

Accommodation (including breakfast)	£55.00
Restaurant (dinner)	£14.95
Bar	£2.25
Conference (per head per day, excluding accommodation)	£35.00

Forward bookings for the next three months are forecasted at approximately 10 per cent below target, and the owners and management are looking closely at costs, especially staffing costs.

As sales and conference manager you have responsibility not only for increasing sales in this area, but also for providing training for staff in customer care and selling skills. While you have been fairly successful in obtaining new business, you have identified that staff lack training in in-house selling skills. You have communicated this to the senior management as an area for positive development.

Prepare a written report for your manager outlining the case for such activity and identifying a brief action plan for consideration.

Exercise No. 12:

Tourist and leisure centre sales and promotion

Croft Craft and Heritage Centre

The Croft Craft and Heritage Centre is situated in a national park. Set in its own grounds, it has a range of retail and leisure facilities attracting a considerable number of visitors.

The buildings spread around the grounds are all operated under one management, although several businesses and outlets are independent. A range of catering facilities is available, including an all-day restaurant, a speciality ice cream shop, and a fast-food outlet. Within this large complex there are also a speciality food shop and a function room available for hire, but the latter is currently underused.

The management is keen to increase the utilisation of the function room and increase customer spend at the various units.

All visitors enter the complex via the main visitor centre, pay a nominal sum for entrance, and receive a printed map of the complex, listing all the facilities.

Consider what methods are available to the management of the centre and which would be most effective in achieving the management's stated aims. Compile a report as follows:

- Make a list of the appropriate methods, with accompanying explanations of how they would be actioned.
- For the function suite, consider a report on ways in which this particular facility can be promoted to visitors.

ADDITIONAL ASSIGNMENT

ASSIGNMENT NO. 7:

A MARKETING AND SALES PLAN

If you consider undertaking this assignment, you are advised to have completed Assignment Nos. 1, 2, 4 and 6. While a marketing plan for the unit could be produced without their completion, the assignments identified would have provided you with a base of appropriate information on which to develop an effective plan.

No marketing consultant or experienced operator would consider preparing a detailed plan without analysis of external factors that may affect the business. This would include competitor and market demand analysis.

An effective marketing plan would draw consideration on both the detailed analysis of the current business performance and potential threats and opportunities. It would lay out in fairly precise terms the activities and actions an operator should undertake to maintain and develop profitable business. Associated with the recommendations would be forecasts of expenditure and expected return.

For newcomers to marketing and sales, this assignment is the most challenging. However, with reasonable access to a unit and reference to aspects of this text and other material, readers should be able to prepare an outline plan.

ASSIGNMENT DETAIL

For a hospitality unit of your choice, prepare a written report detailing the marketing and sales actions you recommend to maintain and develop the operator's business:

- make a list of the activities recommended;
- describe each activity and give reasons for their inclusion;
- give the target market for each activity;
- identify the priorities, listing the activities in order of importance and relevance;
- summarise the key points in a conclusion.

NOTES

- You could also present this plan utilising an overhead projector, accompanied with appropriate additional visual material.
- You are advised to check regularly with the operator during the assignment to ensure the appropriateness of projected ideas.

- Be prepared to produce a rationale for your ideas, for example, if you propose to increase local advertising, why, where and how would this be done.

REVIEW

This section has provided you with examples of marketing and sales challenges. While such activities are utilised to address business needs, they are only part of the picture. Hospitality operators need to ensure they use a broad sweep of other professional management activities. Sound financial control, property maintenance, quality control, staff selection, training and motivation are all just as important.

By compiling the assignments you will quickly identify the importance of such factors and how they interrelate.

The completion of all the assignments would be a major undertaking. However, students of mine have done exactly this and identified considerable benefit from doing so. Individuals should consider the time they have available, the access to an appropriate unit and the relevance of the assignments to their situation.

Good luck with the assignments, take enjoyment in the challenge and satisfaction from their completion.

APPENDIX B:
GLOSSARY

Terms commonly associated with marketing and sales have been utilised throughout this text. The definitions listed below relate to how I have used them and may differ to the standard dictionary definition. I have also included terms not used in this text, which the reader, whether a student, lecturer or professional will come across in the hospitality industry.

Accessibility (of market or products). The degree of ease for which a consumer can access products, services or facilities.

ACORN. Classification of residential areas by the 'type' of people who live in them.

Advertise (verb). To advertise a new product/service/facility.

Advertisement (noun). A notice which shows that something is for sale.

Advertising (noun). The business and practice of announcing something is for sale.

Advertising media. Types of communication used in advertising.

AIDA. Attention, Interest, Desire and Action. A model showing the stages of the desirable effects of advertising on the consumer.

Awareness (noun). Being conscious of an advertising message, or a brand's existence and qualities.

Benefit (noun) – benefit segmentation. The division of a market into segments according to the types of benefits obtained by the customer.

Bipolar scale (noun). A scale used in questionnaires which contains two extreme points within which an interviewee can answer.

Body language (noun). Communication by people utilising gestures or movements of the body.

Boston matrix. A type of product portfolio analysis identifying characteristics of products in relation to cost and demand.

Brand. A make of product/service/facility which can be recognised by name, for example, Harvester, Little Chef.

Campaign. A series of co-ordinated activities designed to reach an objective, for example, sales campaigns, publicity campaigns or advertising campaigns.

Chain. A series or group of units belonging to same company.

Channel. The means by which goods or services or information pass from supplier to customer.

Concept (noun) – marketing concept. A business idea based on the importance of profit and consumer satisfaction.

Consortium (noun). A group of businesses which work together.

Consumer. A person who purchases or utilises goods, services or facilities.

Copy (noun). Publicity copy; text of a proposed advertisement.

Data (noun). Information, letters or numbers available on a computer.

Database. A store of information in a large computer.

Divergent (marketing). Separate marketing treatment for each of a company's products.

Drip (advertising). Placing advertisements for a product of fairly long intervals.

Empirical (data). Data or information that can be proved.

Extrapolation (noun). Forecasting techniques that involve projecting past trends into the future.

Feasibility (study). The careful investigation of a project to see whether it is worth undertaking.

Flagship. A key product or unit in a company's range.

Flow chart. A diagram which shows the sequence of steps in a procedure or plan.

Forecast (sales). The calculation of future sales.

Hype. Excessive claims made in advertising.

Image. The general idea or perception that the public have of a company, unit or product.

Incentive. A thing which encourages a customer to buy.

In-house (selling). The practice of utilising various methods to encourage increased sales or usage.

Jingle. A short or easily remembered tune that is used to advertise a product.

Junk mail. Unsolicited advertising material which is mailed (and often thrown away by the receiver).

Latent (demand). A situation when there exists demand for a product but potential purchases are unable to pay for it.

Lead (sales). Information which may lead to a sale.

Life (cycle of a product). A concept used for charting the different stages in the life of a product.

Logo. The symbol or design used by a company or business as a distinguishing mark on its products, and on its publicity or advertising material.

Loyalty (brand). The inclination of a customer or group of customers to keep purchasing or utilising the same brand of product.

Mail (shot). The process of delivering advertising and promotional material to targeted potential customers.

Marketing (noun). The process of identifying and satisfying customer needs.

Market (analysis). The detailed examination and report on a market.

Market (audit). The detailed investigation of a particular market.

Market (demand). The total demand for a product in the market.

Market (development). The strategy of involving the search for, and exploitation of, new markets.

Market (leader). The company, business or product with the biggest market share.

Market (penetration). The selling of more products into a particular market segment.

Market (research). The examination and investigation of possible sales or the utilisation of a product.

Market (segment). A category of consumers in a market definable by a set of common needs.

Market (segmentation). The division of the market or consumers into certain categories related to purchasing or buying behaviour.

Marketing (mix). The combination of all the elements that make up marketing: product, price, promotion and place, known as the four P's.

Marketing (plan). An annual or period plan for an organisation's marketing activities.

Media. The means of communicating a message.

Merchandising. The display and promotion of goods close to the point of sale.

On-costs. Money spent in producing a product.

Opportunity (sales). An event or factor which provides an opportunity to sell a company's products or services.

OTS – opportunities to see. The number of opportunities an average member of the target audience will have to see an advertisement.

Piggyback (promotion). Sales promotion for one product which accompanies another product promotion.

Portfolio (product). The collection of products, services or facilities offered by one company or unit.

Product (portfolio analysis). The model for developing marketing strategy with various categories of product based on present performance and possible growth rate. Utilised by companies in planning product development and strategy.

Public (relations). Efforts undertaken to create mutual understanding between a company and its public.

Strategy. The plan of future actions.

SWOT (analysis). A method of developing a marketing strategy based upon an assessment of the strengths and weaknesses of the company.

Targeting. Concentrating sales activities on a particular group or market segment.

Telemarketing. Attempting to sell a product or service over the telephone, or conducting research into customer needs by telephone.

Unique (selling point or proposition) or (USP). The special quality of a product that differentiates it from competitors' products.